In the shadow of Pinochet recollections from the resistance against the dictatorship in Chile

Ann Stödberg

In the shadow of Pinochet

recollections from the resistance against the dictatorship in Chile

dedicated to the comrades who gave their lives
in the resistance struggle

Honor and Glory

Publisher: BoD · Books on Demand, Stockholm, Sweden
Printer: Libri Plureos Gmbtl, Hamburg, Germany

ISBN: 978-91-8080-103-4

Table of contents

Preface

I first met Ann at the Kolle-Kolle Conference held outside of Copenhagen in the spring of 1973. This Conference was the inaugural meeting of the Nordic Association for Research on Latin America or NOSALF which had been established with support from the Nordic Council. Despite her youth – she was only 22 – Ann was already a doctoral student at the University of Lund. Her focus was on women in the labor market in Latin America and she participated enthusiastically in both the academic as well as the organizational and social activities.

During the half a century that our paths have crossed since then, I have constantly been reminded of her academic knowledge, her administrative talents and her ability to combine her roles as a parent to small children, a colleague and a friend; something she did with a combination of joy and great seriousness. I have been impressed by her continuous thirst for knowledge, her curiosity regarding new experiences and her social engagement. It's no surprise that Ann, once she retired as a Research Secretary and Manager at the Swedish Agency for Research Cooperation with Developing Countries (SAREC), her final post which followed many years as Country Director for the Swedish International Development Agency (SIDA) in different countries in Africa, Latin America and Asia, now attends courses at Stockholm Seniors´ University, participates in book clubs, is active as a lay judge and is a board member of her housing association. At the same time she dedicates a great deal of time to her successful and internationalized children and grandchildren. As I write Ann is, typically for her, in Boston during some of the summer weeks helping her daughter Isabel get settled in as Isabel starts her doctoral studies at the University of Harvard.

During the fifty years that have passed since our first encounter, I have also got to know Ann as a dedicated feminist and revolutionary, in both senses a true representative for the so-called 68 generation.[1] Her interest and engagement with gender issues runs like a red thread – and I do mean red – throughout the course of her life, ever since her political engagement in the women´s movement as well as her studies in economic history at Lund University when we met in Denmark in 1973, until her position as President of the Board for the NGO Operation 1325,an umbrella NGO for Swedish womens´organizations working to promote peace and conflict resolution processes, which she held for a number of years.

Even if Ann´s work, interests and engagement have been well known among her colleagues and friends, few have had even a glimmer of knowledge about her background as an active member of the underground armed resistance against the military dictatorship under Augusto Pinochet in Chile during the years 1973-1976 and later in Sweden. I feel partially responsible for the fact that Ann´s truly unique and fascinating time together with the leadership for the Chilean Movement of the Revolutionary Left (Movimiento de la Izquierda Revolucionaria – MIR)is now being described by herself. In the beginning of 2022 I gave a brief snapshot of these events in my own biography. Ann has said that it helped her decide to write the text that follows, not least for her own children and grandchildren in order for them to have a more complete picture of their mother and grandmother. There exists an initiative among Chileans in exile to publish both Ann´s story and that of Svante Grände, the son of a Swedish pastor who was in Chile at the time of the military coup and who also joined MIR. After the coup Svante crossed the Andes into Argentina, where he was killed by the Argentinian military in the province of Tucuman in October 1975.

---

1   This refers to the massive student revolt in May 1968 that had a very big influence on young people in that age group in Europe and many other places

In 1973 Ann obtained a scholarship to carry out doctoral studies on women and the labor market in Latin America and, in a situation where the borders had been closed after the military coup and thousands had started to flee, she didn´t hesitate to go against the tide and travel to Chile as soon as the borders opened. When we met in Paris in the days following the coup both I and my friend Charles tried to convince her how dangerous and absurd her intentions were, but she didn´t listen. Ann ,who in Sweden was a member of the Swedish Communist party VPK, planned to contact the Chilean Communist Party. Even in this regard Charles and I tried to deter her, realizing that with her character and her ideological beliefs she was more than likely to wind up reaching out to MIR. Although at that point in September 1973, Ann was doubtful regarding our thoughts, when she finally arrived in Santiago in December, it didn´t take long before she was in touch with MIR and relatively soon after was working with their leadership. From our conversations on the floor of our friend Dani´s apartment in Paris I also remember getting the answer to a question I had been asking myself ever since Kolle-Kolle, which was how she could speak such fluent Spanish; it turned out that she had grown up in Colombia. No doubt this factor was of help to her during her underground life in Chile.

Ann´s story is exhaustive and needs no further clarifications. Apart from my subjective comments on the days in Paris in September 1973, I need to take the opportunity in this short preface, to emphasize my gratefulness for having been able to count Ann Stödberg as well as the father of her children, the MIR leader Mario *Juancho* Espinosa among my dearest friends. In 2023 it will be exactly 50 years since I met Ann. We now live in another world. But when I read her text I think of one of the songs by the Swedish singer song-writer Björn Afzelius, where he describes how we wanted to change the course of history:

" We were the bells in a crucial time. Old friends, come forth! Let me shake your hand! Let me thank you for all we did! We were the future then, and our victories remain, as they do when one has done what one should".

Uppsala July 22, 2022

Tor Sellström

Introduction – Stockholm in September 1973

More than fifty years have passed since September 11, 1973, when Augusto Pinochet overthrew the elected government of President Salvador Allende in one of the most violent military coups in in Latin America. For this reason there is cause to remember what happened and, above all, to remember the brave resistance struggle that took place in Chile against the oppression of the military dictatorship. Many years had to pass before Chile could return to even a limited democracy.

In the following chapters I will explain what I did and what I was a part of from 1973- 1976, when I participated in the resistance movement during the first years of the dictatorship in Chile under Pinochet. This story is based both on my own recollections, letters, documents and newspaper cuttings that I have kept or that have been returned to me, together with information shared with me by several *compañeros* and *compañeras*[2] who were also part of the resistance. I am particularly grateful to Pedro Naranjo Sandoval who fact-checked my text and referred me to other existing documents.[3] Much has been written in Spanish on the dictatorship and the resistance movement. There is some documentation in English and other languages as well. I have used articles and books as well as academic papers as well as information from Chilean public inquiries regarding the dictatorship's victims and the actions of its perpetrators, as well as some of the Chilean Movement of the Rev-

---

2 I will consistently use the Spanish term "compañero" to designate fellow MIR members rather that the term "comrade" which in English is strongly associated with the Communist Party

3 Many of these documents can be found in the electronic archive Archivo Chile (www.archivochile.com) that has been set up by CEME, Centro de Estudios Miguel Enriquez

olutionary Left (Movimiento de la Izquierda Revolucionaria – MIR)'s own internal and public documents from the years mentioned. The photographs are both from the MIR´s archives as well as my own.

The background to my engagement in Chile and the resistance movement lies in my own childhood in Latin America, as well as my student years at the end of the 1960s and the early 1970s. My parents emigrated to Colombia on a freight boat in 1954 with my brother, my elderly grandmother and myself when I was three years old. The reason for my family´s emigration was that my father had travelled abroad extensively as an international sales manager for a large Swedish company in the years following the second world war. He had seen what he considered were great opportunities to start a new life in the New World. He was an engineer by training and was fluent in a number of languages, including Spanish, as well as having a somewhat adventurous nature.

During my childhood in Colombia I witnessed poverty at close hand, and saw how deep class differences led to injustice. During the 1950s and the 1960s , intense and violent clashes between both large landowners and poor farmers in the rural areas, as well as between the working class and the owners of industries in the urban areas, were common in Colombia. The "Fuerzas Armadas Revolucionarias de Colombia", FARC (Revolutionary Armed Forces of Colombia) guerilla was already well established.

In many ways I identified myself as a Latin-American. When I arrived back in Sweden as a sixteen year old, the anti-war movement for Vietnam was very strong and made a deep impression on us high-school students at the time, as did the May 68 revolt in Paris. The Swedish Left grew rapidly, not least in Lund where I was a university student. I lived in a leftwing commune and participated actively in organizations such in Swedish "Vänsterpartiet Kommunisterna",

VPK (the Left Communist Party), and what we had named the Revolutionary Women´s League.

At Lund University I studied political science, sociology and most of all economic history. At that time economic history was the only subject where we could study issues of development and underdevelopment in the so-called Third World. I wanted to understand the social and economic realities in Latin America that I had experienced as a child.

During my years in Chile I never knew the man who later would become the father of my children, *Juancho* (Mario Espinosa Mendez), but I got to know him shortly after he arrived in Sweden in 1976. *Juancho* was a nuclear physicist by training and had joined the MIR in the 1960s. *Juancho* was taken prisoner in 1974 and was subjected to cruel torture before he was finally sent into exile and arrived in Sweden.

I am writing this story for my children and my grandchildren for it is a central part of both my own and Juancho´s lives in Chile and they have a right to know about them. It is also a tribute to those who gave their lives for a free and just society in Chile, and a contribution to ensure that their stories not to be forgotten. For that reason I also wish to share this story with my close friends and compañeros, who are familiar with what happened in Chile during these years, and who participated in resistance and solidarity activities.

Apart from the friendship that united us, Tor, who wrote the preface to this book, and I have shared both political beliefs and engagement. Tor gave his support to the resistance movement through solidarity work in Sweden, and had even, for a brief period in 1973-74, been MIR's representative in Sweden. One month after he wrote the preface, Tor passed away. He had at that point been battling his illness for many years with incomparable willpower.

Chile before and during the Unidad Popular government

It makes sense to take a retrospective look back at the developments in Chile before the military coup. Chile was for a long time considered as a model for democracy in Latin America. At a superficial level the traditional democratic institutions seemed to be working well; elections were held regularly and a parliamentary system was in place; freedom of speech was respected. Yet though there appeared to be a high degree of stability in the political system, violent class antagonisms and confrontations had taken place during the course of history. The institutional reply to these had been oppression. The military and the police forces had been responsible for massacres, abuse and repression; many thousands were killed on different occasions during the last century even before the military coup of 1973. The most infamous massacre was the one that took place in the school Santa Maria de Iquique at the beginning of the 1900´s when more than two thousand Chilean, Bolivian and Peruvian workers and their families, who were demanding better working and living conditions, were cold-bloodedly shot to death by the military. Thus Chile has, throughout its modern history, been characterized by these parallel tendencies; parliamentarism and oppression of powerful social movements[4].

During the sixties there was a surge in the social movements and the Left in Chile, as a result of the growing discontent with high rates of unemployment and economic stagnation. Eduardo Frei Montalva, a leading politician from the center-right "Partido Democrático Cris-

---

4   "Allende´s Chile, the political economy of the rise and fall of the Unidad Popular", Stefan de Vylder

tiano" – PDC (Christian Democratic Party), was elected as President for the period from 1964 – 1970, on a program for social and economic reform. He failed to implement important parts of the reform program. This program was based on the attraction of foreign loans and investments as well as stimulating an import-substitution industry, a model that benefitted the national bourgeoisie. Frei had also taken important steps towards economic and social reforms that his successor, President Salvador Allende could later build on. Frei initiated the nationalization of the copper mining industry; he also started a much-needed agrarian reform and allowed landless farmworkers to organize in trade unions; as well as having promoted maternity centers. At the end of Frei´s presidential period growth had stagnated, unemployment had risen and inflation had increased. At that point, Chile was confronting very big economic and social challenges, at a moment in time when its foreign debt had also grown exponentially.[5] Frei´s politics both provoked confrontations within the ruling class as well as giving rise to mass protest movements among the poorest.

In this context the revolutionary Left grew rapidly, a Left that was inspired by the revolution in Cuba and the guerilla movement in Bolivia. Che Guevara became a powerful symbol. In many corners of Latin America, similar leftist movements gained strength during the same period, for example in Colombia, Uruguay and Brazil. In Chile there already existed a strong working class movement[6] , as well as social mobilization among the urban poor that lived in the shanty towns and landless farmworkers. The student movement was an active driving force in the growing mass movements. Strikes, land occupations, expropriations and other militant actions became more and more common at the end of the sixties. Polarization increased between the leftist forces in Chile, which were primarily composed of parties with reformist pro-

---

5   idem
6   The working class constituted 60% of the population in 1970; see "Chile, mass mobilization and popular power 170-1973 (in Swedish), Tort Sellström

grams, and the national bourgeoisie that was represented both by the conservative right and the Christian Democrat Party.

Salvador Allende, who had been one of the founders of the Chilean "Partido Socialista" PS (Socialist Party), was able to form a coalition among the reformist left-leaning parties in what became the "Unidad Popular" (Popular Unity). The coalition consisted of the Socialist Party, the "Partido Comunista" – PC (Communist Party), the "Partido Izquierda Radical" – PIR (Left Radical Party), the "Izquierda Cristiana" – IC (Christian Left) and the "Movimiento para la Acción Popular Unida" – MAPU (Movement for Popular United Action).

The Unidad Popular coalition stood for election in 1970 with a program focused on the introduction of a "Chilean road to socialism". Allende won the election with only 36,3% of the votes, to a large extent because the conservative forces were split internally. It wasn´t evident that Allende's electoral triumph would be approved by Congress but, in the face of the threat of a civil war, Allende was approved as president.[7] The "Movimiento de Izquierda Revolucionaria – MIR" (Revolutionary Left Movement) chose to remain outside the Unidad Popular governmental coalition and, from the very start, warned of the risk for a military coup d'état.

In the course of the three years that followed, Allende´s ambitious government tried to implement radical structural reforms, characterized as anti-imperialist and anti-monopolist, in an attempt to rectify the extremely unequal distribution of income and power between the classes. The public sector would have a dominating role in the so-called new economy. The economic public sector would be composed of the large scale copper, nitrate, iron and coal mining industries, as well as the financial system, including banks

---

7   de Vylder, idem

and insurance companies, foreign trade, distribution monopolies and strategic industries. The agrarian reform that Frei had initiated would be completed and implemented.[8]

Some of these reforms, such as the nationalization of the large -scale copper and nitrate mining industries, were successful. The national bourgeoisie including important sectors of the middle class as well as the officer corps within the military, mobilized rapidly against Allende. Strikes, lockouts, capital flight and other forms of economic sabotage were used by the rightist forces. Politically the Right organized itself in fascist-type and paramilitary organizations "Patria y Libertad" – PL (Fatherland and Liberty), "Partido Nacional" – PN (National Party) and the reactionary segment of the Christian Democratic Party. Simultaneously workers, small-scale farmers, shanty town[9] dwellers and students mobilized on a grand scale in order to defend measures already taken by the Unidad Popular government and to push for further reforms. This mass mobilization was led in great part by the historic Left, that is the parties that were part of the government coalition, but also by the revolutionary movement MIR. MIR had strong support and grew very fast during the Unidad Popular period. It was a time of many acute and hard confrontations between the mass movements and the reactionary forces in an authentic class struggle. The reactionary forces, with support of the United States Central Intelligence Agency (CIA), were at last able to gain the upper hand.[10]

Allende's Unidad Popular government was overthrown in a military coup on the 11th of September 1973.

---

8   de Vylder, idem
9   In Chile the shanty towns were called "mushroom towns" ("poblaciónes callampas"), which were settlements in informal neighborhoods that sprang up like mushrooms on empty plots outside city limits. They consisted of small constructions of left-over building materials like wood planks, cardboard and in the best of cases tin roofing, and were home to the poorest of the poor.
10   "The Condor Years", John Dinges

Preparations

This story begins in 1973, a year that would be so fatal for so many, particularlyn Chile. For me it was also the year that changed my life forever.

In my student world 1973 had started in a very uneventful way. I lived in Lund which is a small city in the south of Sweden characterized by the centuries-old university, which I was attending. I lived in a commune and could never have imagined what would happen towards the end of that year. I was taking courses in economic history at the initial doctorate level, and was planning to travel to Chile after the summer. I had received a research scholarship from the Swedish International Development Agency (SIDA). I was the only woman in the cohort, and also the only person who would be travelling to Latin America. Latin America was a natural choice since I had grown up there. My goal was to travel to Santiago and do my research at the Latin American Faculty of Social Sciences (Facultad Latinoamericana de Ciencias Sociales – FLACSO), which had academic centers spread across thirteen countries in Latin America.I had been accepted to collect material for my doctoral thesis in economic history. I was planning to write about women in the Chilean labor market between 1950 – 1970, from a a historical perspective. I had made contact with FLACSO in Santiago through Johan Galtung, a Norwegian professor who had worked there and whom I had met in Lund the previous year. That my focus was on Chile was also quite natural, since my interest had been captured by the fact that it had an elected president, Salvador Allende, who was a socialist, and a government, the Unidad Popular, that was implementing a gigantic and radical reform program with a focus on poverty reduction and national ownership of the country´s natural resources. This was extremely unusual in Latin America and, as a left-leaning person myself, I was fascinated. I wanted to be there!

In the spring of 1973 I had the opportunity of attending a major conference in Denmark, in Kolle Kolle close to Copenhagen. The purpose of the conference was to gather researchers from the Nordic countries that were focused on Latin America, and to create an association. That was the start of Nordic Association for Research on Latin America or NOSALF which was established with support from the Nordic Council. Intense discussion took place at the conference regarding different development models and interpretations of development tendencies on the Latin American continent. Chile was of course a hot topic. At the conference I got to know exciting people some of which would later become close friends; among them were Tor Sellström, Agneta Lind and Irene Svensson. All three were planning or already engaged in research on Latin America. Agneta was planning to travel to Chile in September to conduct research on the on-going literacycampaigns modelled on the Brazilian Paulo Freire´s pedagogy which not only taught people to read words, but to read their world through the formation of critical consciousness. Irene was planning to do anthropological research in Peru. Tor, who had studied at the Institute for Latin-American Studies as well as the institute for Political Studies (both in Paris), was going to travel to Chile that same summer to gather material for his doctoral thesis on the agrarian reform in Chile. Tor would later publish the book "Chile, Mass Mobilization and Popular Power 1970-1973" in Swedish. Birgitta Leander who worked UNESCO in Paris and several well-known Latin-American social scientists were also present. The conference was an extremely serious affair but there were also opportunities for more relaxed social activities. It was a bit of a culture shock for the Latin American guests when the Scandinavians proposed joint sauna bathing for men and women together.

As summer was coming to an end I travelled to Stockholm to meet the Swedish development economist, Stefan de Vylder. Stefan had recently returned from Chile where he had spent a year and a half conducting research, and was going to give me an overview of the situation in Chile.[11] Stefan had not attended Kolle Kolle and I knew that it was important for me to have his insights. Stefan was very worried about the situation in Chile, especially because of the so-called "tanquetazo"[12] (tank attack) that had taken place on June 29, 1973 which had been stopped by the constitutionalist army general, Carlos Prats, and his troops. Prats was murdered one year later in Argentina by Pinochet´s secret service National Intelligence Directorate (Dirección de Inteligencia Nacional – DINA) in collaboration with the Argentinian secret service. " El tanquetazo" had led to enormous protests in the whole of Chile, in which some sources estimated that several million people participated. For me, from my Swedish horizon, it seemed as if Allende´s government had very large and strong popular support, and my feeling was that a new attempt at a coup seemed less than probable. It was difficult to make a correct assessment at a distance. Stefan undoubtedly had a better understanding of how critical the situation really was, and thought that it was a bad idea on my part to travel to Chile at the end of August. I didn´t listen. I was so focused on going that I didn´t pay attention to his warning.

I received my International Student ID on September 11, 1973 and my ticket was booked for the following day.

---

11 Stefan published his research in the book "Allende´s Chile, the political economy of the rise and fall of the Unidad Popular", Cambridge University Press, a book which has subsequently been used a course literature in economics
12 The "tanquetazo" was a failed attempt at a coup

Underway

On the evening of September 11, I was packing my suitcase in my commune. I turned on the radio to listen to the news, when I heard that there had been a military coup in Chile and that Salvador Allende was dead. It was a total shock. The military in Chile was generally considered to be a very professional institution with what many had, up until then, believed to be an unfailing loyalty to the constitution. Only a week before, on the anniversary of the presidential election in 1970, almost one million people had demonstrated on the streets of Santiago in support of Allende. So how could this have happened? The image that we had of Chile had been very colored by the Unidad Popular´s own communication messaging and political vision.

I was confused and panicked: what should I do? Should I cancel my trip? I had already sold my furniture and passed on my room in the commune to another person; I had also bid farewell of my friends. There I sat on my bed with my ticket in my hand and my suitcase packed. After thinking it over I decided that I would travel and try and reach clarity during my trip. Maybe I wouldn´t make it to Chile but I could get to Latin America. My ticket took me first to Paris, then to New York and then to my hometown Cali in Colombia. After Cali I was meant to travel on to Santiago. So, my first stop was Paris, where I had already planned to meet Tor who had recently returned from Chile. I was sure he would be able to give me some good advice.

Arriving in Paris the following day I met Tor and his good friend, Charles Achouline, with whom he had travelled in Chile. In Paris students and many others were already out on the streets, vehemently protesting the military coup. Only five years had passed since May '68, and the protests were still fresh in young peoples' minds; it was a natural spontaneous reaction to take to the streets to demonstrate against injustice. Tor, Charles, and I gathered in Birgitta Leander´s apartment (Birgitta´s husband was Chilean) along with others. We tried to obtain information on what was happening in Chile. The news reports were dramatic, and it was evident that the military take-over had been brutal and violent. A state of siege had been declared; the borders were closed; media that had been positive to Allende and the Unidad Popular government had been shut down; and people that the military suspected of being supportive of the Unidad Popular government were being arrested in massive raids. President Allende had died at his post in the presidential palace La Moneda, which had been bombed and set on fire. Much later it would be confirmed that Allende had committed suicide after his last speech to the nation, which had been transmitted on the radio.

All those with family and friends in Chile were attempting to call to find out if they were safe. In the apartment in Paris there was much discussion on what could be done; most were concerned about getting those closest to them, to safety. In the evening an impromptu concert was arranged with the well-known Chilean folk music band Quilapayun which happened to be touring Europe at the time. Quilapayun had been formed in the sixties and was closely associated with Unidad Popular and the movement known as the new Chilean song (Nueva Canción Chilena). The concert took place at the famous Olympia concert hall, and all the Chileans together with people that were sympathetic to Chile who were able to be there, were present. Tor, Charles, and I were there. It was incredibly emotional. People cried and screamed and shouted out the well-known slogan "the people united, will never be defeated ("el pueblo unido, jamás será vencido"). Quilapayun played for many hours, and it seemed as if the concert would never end.

When I left Paris a few days later I didn´t have any more clarity as to what I should do, other than it seemed necessary to do something. What this something would be in concrete terms would later become evident. After a few days stop-over with friends in the U.S. and Colombia, I at last arrived in Peru. At that moment it wasn´t possible to go any further since the borders were closed. My thinking at that point was that I might be able to stay in Peru, if I could get in touch with the University in Lima and see if I could change the focus of my research to Peru instead of Chile; and that maybe I could become a link between those who were preparing solidarity work in Europe and people in need of support in Chile. It is important to add that solidarity groups supporting Latin America and the Unidad Popular government in Chile already existed in many parts of Europe; they had until then been mainly concerned with spreading information about the political situation and advocating support for the process in Chile. I had been a member of such a Latin American solidarity group in Lund.

In Peru I reached out to the University of Lima, but I had no contacts there and there was a complete lack of interest in my research project. After some fruitless attempts I gave up. I decided to wait a while and see how things developed. During this time, I rented a room at the Swedish Seamen´s church. With the help of the Swedish priest, I was able to get a temporary job at an industrial fair that was taking place in Lima at the time, in which some Swedish industries were participating. For a few weeks I worked as a junior hostess for one of these industries – it may have been Volvo -and was able to increase my travel funds which were already starting to diminish. I didn´t want to touch my scholarship money. In Lima I met other Europeans of my age who were travelling around Latin America, and I joined up with some Frenchmen on a hazardous bus trip up to Cuzco at an altitude of 3 400 meters. I became nauseous both from the bus trip as well as the altitude. It took a few days until I was back on my feet again, with the help of coca-leaf tea and rest. We visited the impressive Machu Picchu ruins before returning to Lima, where our paths parted.

I remained in Lima and tried to figure out what my next steps should be. The news from Chile was very worrying. Massive persecution of people, above all from the Unidad Popular, was taking place. Supporters and public servants as well as workers at factories and other workplaces that had been identified by the military were being targeted, as well as known left-wing cultural workers such as singers, writers, actors, and others. Worker neighborhoods and shanty town areas were subjected to extensive raids. Foreigners were also targeted. Tens of thousands were arrested the first couple of months[13] and in Santiago they were, in the beginning, concentrated at the National Stadium. Although these general facts were, to a large extent, known outside Chile´s borders, little was known at a more concrete and detailed level and much information was missing since the military controlled all media – and at that time there was no internet or alternative communication.

Letters and telephone calls were all we had to keep in touch with our contacts in Chile and with the people outside of Chile. As I remember it, I had written to my friends in the Latin America committee in Lund, and they had written back telling me that a person known to them by the name of Tom Alberts was coming to visit Lima soon from Santiago on a work-related mission. Tom was employed as an international expert by the UN Economic Commission for Latin America, ECLA (ECLA in Spanish) and had been working with them for several years. Tom had been there throughout the Unidad Popular government and had witnessed the military coup.

---

13 According to the official inquiry, "Report on Political Arrests and Torture", (the first of the two so-called Valech reports, 2004) calculated that over 22 000 politically motivated arrests were made between September and December 1973

Tom and I met, and what he told me confirmed the loathsome and frightening information about the bloody military persecution of left-wing people that was taking place. This strengthened my determination to contribute in some way to the resistance cause. I discussed this with Tom who, after a time, proposed that I travel to Chile as by then the borders had been opened. The purpose of the trip for me would be to meet and speak to some of Tom´s friends (from both Unidad Popular and MIR) and listen to their possible suggestions and advice. This would give me a basis to form an opinion on whether I could actually contribute in any way, and to take a decision regarding the same. Tom considered that since I had never been in Chile it would not be a problem for me to travel there. Tom also had a reason for this proposal; he needed my help.

During his visit to Lima, Tom had been informed by ECLA that he was not allowed to return to Chile. His contract was close to conclusion and ECLA had decided that he should return directly to Sweden from Peru without first returning to Santiago. Tom was completely opposed to this since he first wanted to sell the house that he had bought in Chile, pack his belongings, and terminate his years in Chile in an orderly fashion. The problem was that, during his stay in Peru, his house had been raided by the military and a gun had been found. Tom had acquired the gun legally and had a license for it. However, the license was in his desk drawer at work and the military was claiming that the gun was illegal. ECLA did not want any problems with the military and had, therefore, decided to prohibit Tom from returning to Chile. Tom´s proposal to me was that I would visit ECLA and request a meeting with ECLA's´ Executive Secretary and Head of Mission, Enrique Iglesias. On Tom´s behalf I would request ECLA's staff to open Tom´s desk drawer and have them deliver the proof of the arm's license to the military, which would clear the way for Tom´s return. In return, I would stay at Tom´s house for as long as he remained in Santiago. That was our deal.

Santiago in December 1973

And that is what happened. On December 4, I took the plane to Santiago. I was terrible nervous of course but did my best to appear calm. I had dressed very carefully in an elegant skirt suit in order to give the appearance of a businesslike young woman. What I didn´t know was that the very same day, the military junta had declared the Swedish ambassador in Chile, Harald Edelstam, to be a *"persona non grata"*, which meant that he was no longer allowed to stay in Chile as a diplomat and had to leave the country as soon as possible.

Ever since the military coup, Edelstam had successfully dedicated himself to saving many people who were persecuted by the military or at risk of being so. How many lives he actually saved is hard to tell, but it was certainly many hundreds. He saved not only Chileans, but also people from Uruguay, Bolivia, Argentina, Brazil, Peru and Ecuador and others, who had been drawn to Chile during the years of the Unidad Popular government. Chile had, since 1970, been a safe haven for left-wing sympathizers. Edelstam´s courage and boldness can´t be exaggerated. His nickname was the "Black Carnation" after his time in Oslo during the Second World War when he had also saved Norwegian lives during the Nazi occupation. On Edelstam´s initiative and with the approval of Olof Palme, Sweden took responsibility for being the international protectorate of Cuba in Chile. In that way the Swedish Embassy could use the Cuban Embassy's office and Ambassador's residence as well as other buildings that were part of the Cuban diplomatic mission. On all of these he raised the Swedish flag to show that the buildings were protected by Swedish diplomatic immunity which meant the military could not, therefore, enter them.

27

In these buildings he placed all the people that needed protection, many of which he personally was able to get out of the National Stadium where they had been imprisoned. Gradually they were evacuated to Sweden, but it took nearly a year before all of them could leave Chile.

Edelstam´s actions were extremely annoying to the military regime and were the reason for his being declared *"persona non grata"* less than three months after the coup d'état.

Edelstam had colleagues at the embassy, among them two young Swedish women, Lilian Indseth and Sonia Martinsson, who continued to take care of the political refugees in the Cuban houses with food and medicine, until they could leave the country, even after Edelstam´s departure. I got to know them both when I arrived in Santiago, especially Lilian who became a close friend. Several years later, Lilian would accompany me at the hospital when my oldest son, Daniel, was born. I never met Edelstam, but I admired him greatly.

Back to Santiago on December 4, 1973. At the airport the border police looked at my visa with a great deal of suspicion. I had obtained my Chilean entry visa at the Chilean Embassy in Stockholm earlier that year. Since it is common practice for Latin American embassies abroad to employ people that are tied to the government in power, it was easy to see that I had obtained my visa from Unidad Popular embassy staff, which in turn made me a suspicious individual. Now I needed to lie fast and convincingly; I assumed the role of an upper-class woman and claimed to be so happy to arrive in Chile at a point in time when there was law and order at last, and that I was very much looking forward to a long planned vacation in Viña del Mar. December is a summer month in the Southern hemisphere and Viña del Mar is a well-known upper-class vacation resort. The border policeman, who evidently had a gullible nature, accepted my explanation, and started to flirt. He asked if I would go to the movies with him! I laughed (nervously) and promised to consider it. So, I passed passport control and could finally get a taxi to Tom´s house.

What I remember of the car ride from the airport into the city, was that there were military patrols everywhere; that the huge avenues were very empty of people and that in many places the word "Jakarta" was painted, in big letters, on the walls. After the coup, the military had rapidly eliminated the colorful wall paintings and messages from the Unidad Popular by painting the walls white. They had let the right-wing message "Jakarta" remain for all to see; a message which was used by the ultra-reactionary right to remind people of the Indonesian genocide of communists that took place in Jakarta in 1965-66. It was thus a message from the right to the military, spurring them on to do the same in Chile.

From 1970 the reactionary, right wing forces in Chile had received support from the CIA. The extent of this support later emerged through the ample documentation made public many years later[14]. These forces also had support from an important part of the military leadership, which planned and executed the bloody coup that was finally carried out on September 11, 1973. Stefan de Vylder had told me about the attempted coup or "tanquetazo" that had taken place in June 1973. While this attempt failed it had, in practice, made it possible for the reactionary forces to identify the constitutionalists in the military that were opposed to a coup, among them General Carlos Prats. These troops and officers had been isolated and neutralized by the coup plotters shortly before the successful coup took place in September. Many were arrested and a great many

---

14   This documentation was made public by the Clinton administration, see for example "The Condor Years " by John Dinges

of them were later court-martialed and executed. General Prats, who had resigned a month earlier and been replaced by Pinochet as Commander in Chief of the Army, fled to Argentina. Prats was subsequently assassinated the following year.

Having arrived at Tom´s house in the middle-class neighborhood of Nuñoa, I was received by Anita, Tom´s housekeeper. I explained the situation to her and started preparing myself for my first task: to go to ECLA and request a meeting with ECLA's Executive Secretary, the Uruguayan economist Enrique Iglesias. After a few days I was able to do this, which led to permission for Tom to return to Santiago and prepare his move back to Sweden.

One afternoon, before Tom had returned, the doorbell rang. This happened about a week after my arrival in Santiago. Anita had already told me that a good friend of Tom´s had been stopping by and would surely turn up any day. At the door I met a man with a pencil mustache, properly dressed in a business suit, with glasses and combed back hair. From the description given to me by Tom I knew who he was; his political name was *Eduardo,* and he was a MIR militant.

Eduardo changed his political name many times during the period that I knew him: he also called himself *Diego*, *Omar* among other names. His last political name was *Quintullanca*, a Mapuche[15] name.

Much, much later I learned by chance that *Eduardo* was Dagoberto Perez and that he was the Head of MIR's regional committee for Santiago and a member of MIR's Central Committee.[16] From here

---

15 Mapuche is an indigenous people in Chile
16 MIR was a nation-wide organization and consisted of both local committees in smaller communities and of GPM (political-military groups) in larger

on I will only call him Dago, as he was known to his family, his clos-est friends and *compañeros,* for the sake of simplicity. It should be mentioned that MIR had taken a decision that all contacts with foreigners should be broken off after the coup, for safety reasons. The reasoning was that foreigners could be easily identified and could, in worst case scenarios, lead to the security forces to MIR members. Dago was thus breaking a rule, but he had a good reason to do so.

I was very happy to meet Dago since it was my first contact with the resistance movement. Dago was very suspicious of me and wondered who I was. I rapidly explained the situation with Tom and that he would soon be returning. I told him that the purpose of my trip was to gain a better understanding of the general situation in order to assess if there was anything I could contribute with to the resistance struggle. If anything, this made Dago even more suspi-cious. He told me to get into his car. If I remember correctly was a small inconspicuous car, maybe a Renault-4 or a small Citroen, which were very common cars in Santiago at the time. Without further ado and without saying any more, he drove far outside of the city limits. He finally stopped on a country dirt road without any people or houses in sight. Then began a long interrogation which lasted hours.

---

communities that were in their turn organized in geographically defined regional committees. At the time of the coup there existed eleven regional committees where Santiago was the largest and most important. Apart from these structures, there were central functions separate from the GPM and the regional committees. The highest level of decision making was the party congress that elected the members to the Central Committee. The Central Committee in its turn elected eight to the executive body, the Political Commission (Comisión Politica). The Political Commission had a secretariat and the entire organization was led by the Secretary General.

Dago holding a speech in his capacity as a student leader,
before the coup

Dago wanted to know everything about me, who I was, why I had
come to Chile, what I really wanted, how come I spoke such good
Spanish, and if I had any clue at all as to what had happened in
Chile the past months. I explained about my childhood in Colombia;
how I had seen deep class differences and poverty; that as a child
I had witnessed how general Rojas Pinilla had governed Colombia
through dictatorship during the fifties, and how he was removed
through massive popular protests in 1957. I also told him about
how I had lived in Madrid during Franco and had seen how leftist
students had been persecuted by military police. I explained that
I had arrived back in Sweden as a sixteen-year-old and after high
school graduation studied sociology and later for Master's degree
in economic history, which was the equivalent to the first step to a

Ph.D., at the University of Lund. I explained that I had obtained a scholarship to carry out research at FLACSO and had been planning to come to Chile much earlier but had postponed my travel to finish some courses. I also explained that I was a member of Swedish Left Communist Party (VPK) and a group that carried out solidarity work with Latin America.

When I mentioned my membership in VPK, Dago again became dubious, since MIR was very critical of the Chilean Communist Party. In Chile there had long been an ideological conflict between MIR and the Chilean Communist Party. There were many political differences between the two. On the one hand there was a vast difference in their analysis of the situation in Chile. The Chilean Communist Party (PC) considered Chile to be a feudal country. MIR did not. MIR considered Chile to be a neo-colonial, underdeveloped capitalist country that had a relationship of dependency vis a vis developed countries, particularly the U.S.[17]

This was much more than a mere academic issue because it determined their choice of key strategic alliances. While the PC strongly supported a reformist policy and sought alliances with political forces in the center to bring about change, MIR considered that armed struggle was necessary. MIR also considered the PC to be a Stalinist party, due to its open support of the invasion of Czechoslovakia by the United Socialist Soviet Republic (USSR) in 1968. The PC, in turn, considered MIR to be a "petit bourgeois" movement made up of revolutionary romantics. Dago and I had a long discussion that day where I explained that the Swedish VPK had rejected Stalinism and that the Swedish Communist Party was very different organization to the Chilean PC.

17 According to the Dependency Theory that had been developed by the German economic-historian Andre Gunder Frank and his Brazilian economist colleague Ruy Mauro Marini who was also a member of MIR

At last Dago seemed to accept my explanations. At a later point he told me that his biggest doubt was whether I was possibly some kind of foreign agent, maybe even a CIA spy, with a Swedish cover. At last, he accepted that I was probably no more than a than a very naïve young Swedish girl, but that I had honest intentions. I kept repeating that I wanted to contribute in some way to the resistance struggle, and that it was up to him to assess that and suggest what I could do. It should be said that I had planned to make the same "offer" to the other Left parties and hear what they replied, since it was not all clear to me at the beginning that I should work with the MIR. This part I did not mention to Dago, of course.

Perhaps it was the fact that I had no past in Chile, so I was not "quemada" or "burnt", i.e. not identified by the security forces, and that I had an unusual but nevertheless legitimate reason to be in the country, that led to Dago accepting that he would consider my proposal. We would meet again when he had had time to think about it. He also gave me some good advice: that I should forget FLACSO, where the military already had arrested a number of foreigners. This proved to be quite correct since FLACSO, when I eventually got in touch with them, immediately told me that, under no circumstances, could I work there. The situation for foreign students and researchers was much too dangerous. Much later I learnt that Dago himself had worked at FLACSO as a young sociologist. Dago suggested that I contact some of the other international organizations in Santiago, of which there were a number, to see if they would give me a workplace. I don´t think we discussed any specific institute that day, but I clearly remember that, if I was to be of any use to MIR and to the resistance movement, it was important that I had a legitimate workplace.

Dago drove me back to Tom´s house and I didn´t see him again until Tom had returned to Santiago. As a final control, Dago wanted to hear from Tom, whom he had known for some years, to see if my story checked out. During the weeks that followed I also met other acquaintances of Tom within the Left; among them were socialists, communists, MAPU-supporters, and members of the Christian Left. In the conversations with them it became evident that all of those that were sympathetic to or members of parties within the UP, considered that it was a hopeless situation and that it would be impossible to put up any resistance to the junta, given that the power of the military dictatorship was total and their persecution merciless. They considered that the only possible action was to seek political asylum with those embassies that didn't recognize the junta. The parties encouraged those members who feared for their lives to seek asylum. As a result, numerous European embassies, as well as some Latin-American embassies that did not at the time have military dictatorships, were rapidly filled with asylum seekers. The only party that had a policy to actively promote and carry out resistance actions against the military dictatorship, was MIR. Consequently, it was with MIR and the "Movimiento de Resistencia Popular – MRP" (Popular Resistance Movement), that I wanted to work.

One can wonder why I chose to stay in Chile and work with the resistance and MIR. There were several reasons for that decision. On the one hand, with my leftist political convictions, I felt that I had an unusual and unique possibility to contribute, albeit in a modest fashion, to a necessary and just struggle. At this point in time, "international solidarity" were words of honor. On the other hand, my "Latin American identity" also meant that Chilean cause was mine as well. I suppose that the arrogance typical of youth also played a role. I was fairly aware, in any case, of the possible consequences.

The period between September and December 1973 had been characterized by mass arrests of both representatives of the UP government and public servants at all levels, as well as ordinary citizens that were UP sympathizers. People were openly gunned down on the streets and, during the first days after the coup, bodies were seen floating in the Mapoche river that ran through Santiago.

Naturally none of this was reported by the right-wing Chilean newspapers and all media that were sympathetic to the UP had been shut down immediately. So, nothing was said of the mass arrests on the television or radio. I had heard about them before arriving in Chile but once there, there was a complete media silence. We would have needed the internet…. However, I read the newspapers and was made aware of the intense hate propaganda against the Left and the supporters of Allende´s government that was published every day. I particularly remember the hate-filled articles about Ambassador Edelstam; it was stated that he represented a communist country and that the Swedish Prime Minister Olof Palme, was a messenger boy for Moscow. There was a campaign to change the name of the street called Suecia (Sweden). I also listened to the radio and the first time I heard Pinochet speak I took it for an odd joke. His nasal voice and uneducated way of expressing himself seemed like a caricature of the man himself – how was it possible? – until I understood that it was actually Pinochet speaking. Pinochet was convinced that God had given him the mandate to "save the country".

I was scared to go out on the streets and remember that at that time, I would limit myself to accompanying Anita to the local farmer´s market. I remember the tense expression on people´s faces. There was fear everywhere and it was like a heavy wet blanket over the city, and for that matter, over the entire country. Christmas and New Year´s Eve must have come and gone, but I don´t remember any of it.

MIR and the Resistance Movement

MIR was founded in 1965 and unified different left – wing organizations that believed that real change in Chile would only be possible through a revolutionary seizure of power. MIR's analysis was that the reformist, electoral path to power would never be able to achieve the profound changes in Chilean society were needed to ensure social justice for all Chilean people. MIR, therefore, took the decision not to participate in the Unidad Popular leftist electoral alliance which stood behind Salvador Allende for ideological reasons. MIR had no confidence that the reactionary forces in the country would allow Allende´s policy of democratic socialism to be carried out. In the end, their assessment proved to be correct. Before the elections in 1970 there was an internal discussion on whether members should vote or not vote for Allende, and there were different positions. Finally it was decided that everyone could decide to do as they best saw fit.

After the military coup, MIR made many efforts to unite the Left in a resistance struggle against Pinochet´s dictatorship. MIR's political platform after the coup had four goals: 1) to restore all democratic rights and freedoms as well as the respect for human rights; 2) to restore and defend the living standard of the vast majority; 3) to organize and develop the popular resistance movement; and 4) to overthrow the military dictatorship and install a new government. [18] This platform resonated strongly with me.

Apart from myself there was also another Swede who had chosen to stay and work with MIR. We never met. He was Svante Grände

---

[18] See "MIR, dos años en la en la lucha de la resistencia popular del pueblo chileno 1973–75", MIR

who, at the time of the coup, was in the south of Chile. Svante had gone to Chile with the Swedish NGO Training for Development Work (UBV) but, once there, he had joined MIR. Compañeros from MIR participated in an armed attack immediately after the coup, on a police station in Neltume in the southern region of Los Lagos region, close to where Svante was. The attack failed and led to the arrest of several of the members in the group. They were later executed. Svante managed to escape and to cross the Andes on foot to Argentina. Once in Argentina Svante joined the Argentinian guerilla organization, the People´s Revolutionary Army (Ejército Revolucionario del Pueblo – ERP).[19] Svante´s political name was Teniente Julio. Svante was killed in battles between the ERP and the Argentinian army in Tucuman in 1975. He was 28 years old, and his body has never been recovered.

Besides Svante, to my knowledge, there were no other Swedes who worked directly with MIR in the resistance struggle after the coup. MIR had members from other countries that had joined the party before the coup; most of them were Latin-Americans but there were also one or two North Americans and some Europeans. The foreigners within MIR had permission to leave Chile after the coup and many went to Argentina.

In 1972 the different revolutionary organizations in the Southern Cone[20] of Latin America began to build fraternal links and share experiences. The initiative had been taken by the secretary general of MIR, Miguel Enriquez and brought together MIR in Chile, the

---

19 In accordance with the agreement within the JCR – the revolutionary coordinating committee that was integrated by MIR in Chile, the PRT-ERP in Argentina, the MLN-Tupamaros in Uruguay and the ELN in Bolivia. More on the JCR in the following footnotes below
20 Traditionally the Southern Cone consists of Chile, Argentina, and Uruguay, sometimes also including Paraguay. In the case of the JCR, it included Chile, Argentina, Uruguay, and Bolivia

"Partido Revolucionario de Trabajadores – Ejército Revolucionario del Pueblo or PRT-ERP" (Revolutionary Workers Party – People's Revolutionary Army)[21] in Argentina and the "Movimiento Nacional de Liberación Tupamaros – MLN-Tupamaros" (National Liberation Movement Tupamaros)[22] in Uruguay. The "Ejército Nacional de Liberación – ELN" (Bolivian National Liberation Army)[23] joined in 1973. In August 1973, one month before the military coup in Chile, the "Junta Coordinadora Revolucionaria – JCR" (Revolutionary Coordinating Committee) was formally established as an alliance between the above-named four organizations. Those that signed for their respective organizations were the General Secretary of the MIR, Miguel Enriquez and his brother Edgardo Enriquez, Roberto Santucho, the General Secretary of the PRT-ERP, Efraín Luis Martinez and William Whitelaw for the MLN-Tupamaros leadership and Osvaldo "Chato" Peredo and Ruben Sanchez for the ELN. [24]

The JCR wasn´t just an ordinary run-of-the-mill alliance or a merger of the member organizations. In its first public declaration "To the People of Latin America", the JCR called for a joint anti-imperialist struggle for socialism across the Latin-American continent. In the declaration it said that the revolutionary struggle is a complex process of mass struggle and can be both armed and unarmed; peaceful and violent, in which all the different forms of struggle are developed harmoniously and come together to reinforce the armed struggle.

The purpose of the JCR was not only to inspire and influence, but also very practical. The JCR aimed build a joint infrastructure for

---

21 The Argentinian part of JCR consisted of the PRT (Revolutionary Workers Party) that had been founded in 1965, later a military branch was formed, the ERP (the People´s Revolutionary Army)
22 MLN-Tupamaros was the Uruguayan Movement for National Liberation, founded in 1963
23 ELN was the National Liberation Army in Bolivia and was founded in 1967
24 Source: The Condor Years by John Dinges (2004)

mutual logistic, financial, and military support between the revolutionary organizations in Latin America. One of the agreements was that the member organizations should conduct the struggle in their countries according to their own methods and their own timetables. Each organization should determine when and how the armed part of the struggle should be initiated. The members could participate and fight in each other's organizations. Joint military and ideological training was offered.

A few years later the military dictatorships in Chile, Argentina, Uruguay, Paraguay and Bolivia, backed by the CIA, created a counter-organization – Operation Condor – to crush the JCR and its member organizations.[25] More on the Operation Condor further on.

The military coup on the 11th of September was brutal, bloody, and excruciatingly thorough. All branches of the military forces in the army, the navy, and the air force together with the Carabineros police force, participated and acted in a totally coordinated way. The coup was led by Augusto Pinochet who had, ironically, been appointed by Allende as Commander-in-Chief of the army only 18 days before the coup.

The armed forces acted against the population like an invading foreign power. Martial law was declared; congress was closed, and all civil rights and freedoms were terminated. The military's position was that they were conducting a war, a war against the Left. The orders were to crush the UP and its sympathizers. Soon MIR, the so-called extremists, were also targeted. The coup took the form of state terrorism against the population. Little did we realize at the time that the dictatorship would last for seventeen long years.

---

25 Idem

The few pockets of resistance that took place the first day of the coup were rapidly put down by the military. One of the first took place in the industrial area Cerrillos in the outskirts of Santiago. Some of the MIR leaders – Miguel Enriquez, Bautista van Schouwen, Arturo Villavela and Andres Pascal Allende – met at the INDUMET factory with leaders from the Socialist Party in the afternoon of the 11th. The purpose of the meeting was to agree on what actions to take jointly against the military. Many of the factory workers were present. The Socialist Party rejected the proposal to make armed resistance because they wanted to wait and see what other measures the military were going take apart from the bombing of the Moneda. Meanwhile the factory was soon attacked by military and police, and both the MIR and Socialist Party leaders had to defend themselves with the arms they were carrying. They narrowly escaped being captured but there were heavy losses on both sides, among them, on the part of MIR, the ex-member of the GAP *"Léon"* (Manuel Ojeda Dissikon) who lost his life that day.

According to Carmen Castillo, the compañera of Miguel Enriquez, in the morning of the 11th Miguel had tried to reach Allende by telephone in the Moneda but had only been able to speak to his daughter Beatriz who was there with him. Miguel offered to mobilize the MIR forces and rescue Allende, and help him go underground. Allende rejected that proposal and sent the following message back, through Beatriz: "Now its your turn Miguel. I´m not going anywhere."

The constitutionalist military forces had been neutralized by the high commanders before the coup and they couldn´t act. Before the 11th of September, MIRs' previous assumption had been that the constitutionalist troops would lead the defense of the democratic government, but this had been prevented by the instigators of the coup. So that option was discarded as a line of defense. The massive and coordinated military action on the first day of the coup completely outnumbered the few armed units within MIR and, together with the fact that no other parties on the Left were willing or minimally prepared to take part in armed defense actions, led MIR to the conclusion that armed resistance was not viable at that point. So Miguel Enriquez, after a consensus decision made by the Political Commission, gave the order already on the evening of September 11th that MIR should retreat and not engage in any further armed resistance actions, until further notice. However, not even the leaders of MIR had any notion at that point that the coup and the repression that followed would be so totally devastating.

Since MIR had knowledge that a coup was imminent, a standing order had already been given that, in the event of a coup, all members of the party should go underground ("pasar a la clandestinidad"). [26]

To go underground, in concrete terms, meant that each and every one should change his or her appearance ("enmascararse") as far as possible; men should shave off their moustaches, sideburns and/ or beards (many had big moustaches); hair should be cut and/or dyed; business attire should be used and new, false identity papers should be used. Everybody should move to safe houses and only communicate with other compañeros and compañeras following pre-established protocols. For the most part, this implied that work was re-organized so that it would be carried out in small units of two or three persons at the most; only information that was strictly necessary for the work to be carried out, was shared (compartmentalization or "compartimentacion" in Spanish); all correspondence or documents were written and sent in the smallest possible format, sometimes in microfilm or on roll of cigarette paper, that was hidden in innocent household articles like spaghetti packages. Women were to use make-up, dress in skirts or dresses and change their

---

26   Information shared by Pedro Naranjo Sandoval

hairstyles as well as moving to safe houses and follow the rest of the safety instructions.

These instructions and preparations had taken place before the coup since, as mentioned earlier, MIR had previously been informed of the imminent risk of a coup by non-commissioned officers in the army loyal to the constitution. This knowledge had also been shared with Allende, but neither he, nor the rest of the UP, took it seriously. There is credible information that Allende wanted to announce a referendum regarding support for his government and had set the date for the announcement for September 11 or 12. Allende was prepared to resign if the referendum went against him. The date for the coup was determined by this plan for a referendum which the military wanted to prevent at all costs[27].

It should be pointed out that this was not the first time that MIR had gone underground. This had already occurred in 1969 when the party had been persecuted during the Christian Democrat government of Eduardo Frei. On that occasion the persecution had, above all, targeted certain sectors of MIR in Santiago and Concepción. The persecution led to the arrest of a number of MIR members who remained in jail for months. Dago had been among them. Lessons had been learnt regarding what a life underground required.

When MIR went underground after the coup there was need for helpers ("ayudistas"). They were people who were not members of MIR but sympathetic to the cause, as well as the so-called "links" ("enlaces") who were people who were members of MIR, but unknown to the police and secret services. The "links" could go around openly and could carry out support tasks such as setting up safe houses, transporting messages and other tasks that those who were underground were unable to do.

---

27 Archivo Chile (CEME)

The intense political mobilisation during the years that preceded the Unidad Popular led to a number of MIR members being jailed, later to be pardoned by Allende. Top row from the right is Dagoberto Perez, besde him José Bordas Paz, Alejandro de la Barra and José Benado. Bottom row, third form the right is Chico Zorilla, fourth is Sergio Perez and fifth is Jorge Espinosa (*Juancho*´s brother).

MIR's Political Commission, which was composed of eight members from the Central Committee, took a joint decision that MIR members should remain in Chile and fight against the dictatorship. The slogan was "MIR does not seek asylum". There were two strong reasons for this decision. The first was that the coup itself, being a violent political setback, required the Left to retreat and that the retreat needed to be conducted in an orderly way. This could only happen if the parties or a party on the Left remained in the country. The other reason was that the vast majority of the population, that is the working class, the small farmers, and the poor in the shanty towns, was unable to seek asylum and had to remain in the country. So, MIR considered that it was both a strategic issue related to how the continued fight against the dictatorship should be conducted and a class issue. It was a question on taking sides with the most vulnerable. MIR considered that to seek asylum was to betray the struggle. The most important task was to create a people´s resistance movement, the "Movimiento de Resistencia Popular" – MRP (Popular Resistance Movement).

The decision to not allow asylum as an option for anyone in MIR was heroic and it had a very strong symbolic value when it was taken. However, in hindsight, both myself and others have come to the conclusion that it was erroneous. Of course, we didn´t realize it at the time. Several of the surviving MIR compañeros and compañeras later conceded that MIR should have evacuated the most persecuted, the most important and most experienced leaders. Many valuable lives could have been saved if the party had been more flexible and pragmatic. In practice a number of MIR members did leave the country during the coming years, mainly when they saw no other way of saving their own lives or those of their families. Most of those who left Chile did so after having been released from jail or from concentration camps. A release from jail or concentration camp was no guarantee for not being arrested again or simply "disappeared".

MIR's organizational structure consisted of a nucleus of party members together with sympathizers from a number of groups from different social sectors across the whole country. These groups were organized into the so-called fronts or "Frentes" in Spanish, which were loosely constituted sector-based groups led by MIR members. After MIR was founded in Santiago in 1965, its social base grew. This growth was most rapid during the UP years. MIR conducted dedicated and focused work in the different sectors. Gradually nation-wide coverage was achieved although the strongest base was in Santiago and in the southern regions of the country. The national-level fronts consisted of the Front of Revolutionary Students (Frente de Estudiantes Revolucionarios, FER) that was made up of university as well as high school students[28]; the Movement of Revolutionary Farmers (Movimiento de Campesinos Revolucionarios, MCR); the Movement of Revolutionary Shanty Town Dwellers (Movimiento de Pobladores Revolucionarios, MPR); and the Revolutionary Workers´ Front (Frente de Trabajadores Revolucionarios, FTR).

MIR also had organizational support among progressive military officers and troops but unlike the sector fronts that were open and public, these structures were secret and highly compartmentalized.

At the time of the UP government, if all those that were active in these fronts together with sympathetic grass- roots or base movements are included, MIR had an outreach or sphere of influence of 30,000 to 50,000 people.[29] MIR' strongest base existed within the student movement, the small farmers movement and the shanty town dwellers.

MIR was a party of cadres, made up of small groups of trained activists who could assume leadership and train others. In contrast the Communist and the Socialist parties were mass parties. Thanks to this structure and its relationship with the Fronts, MIR had an influence that was much greater than the number of its members in comparison to similar parties at the time, both in Chile and more widely in Latin America.

At the time of the military coup, MIR had around 10,000 members when all levels of membership were included[30]. According to a cal-

---

28 The Movement of University Students of the Left (Movimiento de Universitarios de Izquierda, MUI) was a student movement that had been formed previously and that later was integrated into FER.
29 In accordance with a conversation between myself and Andres Pascal Allende in August 2022
30 Idem. This included "sympatizantes", "aspirantes" and "militantes"

culation that Dago made soon after the coup, between 5,000 – 6,000 were fully fledged combatants ("militantes") which was the highest level of membership; in Santiago alone, there were around 2000 "militants".[31]

It was very important that the helpers could assist with legal facades for the *compañeros* and *compañeras*. The function of a "Palo Blanco" (literally "White Stick") – a person who was "above ground" and who could act as a facade for a *compañero* who was underground – was particularly important. This function was especially useful in setting up safe houses. The "Palo Blanco" would hire a house or apartment and the compañero or compañera who was underground would live and or work there. This function had already existed before the coup, but it became an essential part of MIR's safety structure afterwards. This was the reason why Dago had insisted that I have a convincing and legal facade so that I could be a Palo Blanco for him. When he and I agreed that I would work with MIR and the Popular Resistance Movement, I was given my first political name, *Isabel*. Later I would change my name to *Claudia*. I will explain further on what tasks I was given, but firstly some information about the context in Santiago in December 1973.

In December, when Edelstam was declared "*persona non grata*" Pinochet´s secret police service, the National Intelligence Directorate (Dirección de Inteligencia Nacional – DNA) had already begun to function *de facto*. The DINA was formally created in November of 1973, and has often been called Pinochet´s Gestapo. It was led by Manuel Contreras from the Tejas Verdes regiment. Many years later, Contreras was put on trial and condemned for the assassination of Allende´s former foreign minister, Orlando Letelier, in Washington

---

31 In accordance with a conversation between myself and Patricio Rivas *(Gaspar)* in August 2022. The numbers have also been confirmed by Mario Espinosa *(Juancho)* and Pedro Naranjo *(Mario)*.

in 1976. Some years later his sentence was increased to 526 years for kidnapping, assassination, and disappearance of Left militants.

Contreras was responsible for the infamous Villa Grimaldi in Santiago, which was one of the places where the DINA brought those that had been taken by them, and where they were mostly tortured to death. To be taken by the DINA was almost always equivalent to a death sentence. Other infamous torture centers were Londres 38 and the Cuartel Ollague on the street José Domingo Cañas. The first prisoner to die in Villa Grimaldi was apparently the medical doctor Bautista van Schouwen, who had been betrayed by a Spanish priest. He was arrested on December 13, 1973, and was subjected to terrible torture. He died soon afterwards, probably on the following day. Bautista, whose nickname was "Bauchi", was one of MIR's historic founders and the second in command after Miguel Enriquez in MIRs Political Commission[32]. The *compañero* Patricio Munita who had been arrested together with Bautista van Schouwen, was tortured to death on the same occasion. Bautista van Schouwen was 30 years old and Patricio Munita 23 years old when they were assassinated. MIR quickly realized that van Schouwen had been arrested but it took a long time to get clarity in his fate.

---

[32] The people who made up the Political Commission at the time of the coup were Miguel Enriquez (MIRs General Secretary), Bautista van Schouwen, Edgardo Enriquez, Andrés Pascal Allende (Allende´s nephew), Nelson Gutierrez, Roberto Moreno, Arturo Villavela and Humberto Sotomayor. There was an internal hierarchy between the first four in this order. Of those in the Political Commission at the time, only three are alive today. Edgardo Enriquez became head of MIR outside of Chile when, by a consensus decision, it was decided by the Political Commission that he should leave Chile in order to take on that task.

The first period

In January Tom prepared his move back to Sweden. By this time Dago and I had agreed that I would start contributing to the resistance by carrying out some specific tasks. Dago asked me to rent a small apartment in a middle-class area. This proved to be easy since many people were leaving Chile, maybe not because of persecution but more out of generalized fear, and wanted to rent out their apartments or houses. So I soon found and rented a fully furnished one-bedroom apartment on the Avenida Santa Maria, which was on the other side of the Mapocho river from where I had been staying up until then. I was able to move in at the end of January. The apartment would be a safe house serving as a meeting place for Dago and those who worked closest with him.

I also had some other tasks, like changing money. MIR received US dollars from abroad, mainly from the PRT, MIR´s sister organization in Argentina, as part of the cooperation with the JCR. It was impossible,of course, to go to a bank or money exchange office, since the sums were considerable and would have been suspicious. Luckily this wasn´t hard either. I turned to Tom´s work colleagues at ECLA and their friends. Many of them were locally employed Chileans who wanted to leave the country and needed dollars without having to go to a bank. I made up incredible stories to justify having so much money; that I had a rich father and that I had decided to settle down in Chile and wanted to buy property; or that I had recently inherited a lot of money that I wanted to invest in Chile; that I was buying a house or a car. The stories weren´t very credible but no one bothered to ask questions. Those who wanted dollars and had pesos weren´t interested in knowing why I had so much money in cash. Changing the dollars to pesos was an important task and could in practice only be carried out, without alerting the authorities, by foreigners. I assumed that Dago´s friendship with Tom had perhaps a similar origin. Changing money was one of my major tasks for the first months.

Another task was to ride with Dago in the passenger seat of his car to give the impression of a normal couple, while he picked up different compañeros y compañeras, one at a time, and had short meetings with them in the car. It was supposed to look innocent and normal, just a man and a woman driving around in a car, at times with another passenger in the back seat. That became my first experience of being a façade.

It was clear from the beginning that Dago had some kind of important role, since it was obvious that he was giving the orders, but I couldn´t guess what these conversations were about more specifically. It might appear that it was naïve to have me come along and to listen to what was being said, but actually I didn´t understand anything. I did speak fluent Spanish but Chilean Spanish is very special. On the one hand it can be spoken very rapidly, cutting out the end syllables – Dago was an expert – but he also used Santiago slang which was incomprehensible to an outsider. That was the way Dago spoke with the compañeros for security reasons. I could ride around in the car for hours and witness several brief – no more than ten minute – meetings but not understand anything of what was said. It wasn´t because Dago didn´t trust me but because of the general rule, which was never to have any more information than was absolutely necessary. Sometimes Dago met people more regularly and I learned to recognize them. One such person was *Gaspar*, whom I met for the first time in my apartment on Avenida Santa Maria and where Dago could have longer meetings.

By January 1974 MIR had succeeded in going underground and up to that moment, with a few terrible exceptions such as Bautista van Schouwen and Patricio Munita, the losses had been relatively few. There was a certain feeling of relief, and that focus could now shift to the new tasks that were needed to build the resistance movement. This feeling soon proved to be mistaken, for the intense persecution of MIR had only just begun.

In April eight members of MIR's Central Committee that had been working in the southern regions of the country were arrested, together with some other key members of the party. I was soon to learn that within MIR we didn´t really talk about being caught or arrested, but instead of "falling" ("caer" in Spanish). This was because being "caught" or "arrested" implied that it was a legitimate and legal action on the part of the authorities, and that it would be documented. However, that was not the case with the persecution carried out by the security services working for the dictatorship. To "fall" meant detention in secret places, arbitrary torture and often disappearance/ death.

Gaspar (Patricio Rivas) who worked closely with Dago, was arrested in June 1974 and it would take years before I met him again. *Gaspar* fell into the hands of the Air Force Intelligence Service (Servicio de Intelligencia de la Fuerza Aérea – SIFA), not Pinochet's DINA. At this time there were strong clashes between Gustavo Leigh Guzman, who was Commander in Chief of the Air Force and Pinochet, as the Commander in Chief of of the Army. This antagonism was also reflected in the actions their respective secret services. Pinochet´s DINA frequently tortured their prisoners to death. Almost all the people who were "disappeared", and who were never found either dead or alive, were taken by DINA. According to official sources around 1200 people were "disappeared", mostly from MIR and the Socialist Party. SIFA also tortured its prisoners, using vicious physical abuse, isolation and mock executions and showed no mercy but, in contrast to DINA, it did not kill them. However, the torture imparted by SIFA left life-long physical and/or psychological scars.

Juancho (Mario Espinosa), subsequently the father of my children whom I never met while in Chile, was captured by SIFA forces in September 1974. He was held prisoner in the basement premises of the Academy of Air War (Academia de Guerra Aérea – AGA) for over six months together with *Gaspar* and other MIR members[33]. *Juancho* was a member of the MIR Central Committee, where he had contributed to the build-up of the party´s operations activities. During the Frei government in the sixties *Juancho* took part in the planning and execution of several acts of expropriation in the form of bank robberies. The money that was taken in these actions was used to buy and distribute essential items such as food to shanty town population, as well as reinforcing MIR's own supply of cash. In solidarity with Allende and the UP government no bank robberies were carried out between 1970-1973.

The MIR members that received guerrilla/military training became the nucleus of MIR´s "Central Force" (Fuerza Central – FC) which was headed by *Juancho*. Some of those that participated in the Central Force had earlier been a part of Allende's personal security detail, the Grupo de Amigos del Presidente (The Friends of the President) known as GAP. The GAP was initially made up of only MIR members, at the request of Allende.

Arturo Villavela, whose political name was *Coño Aguilar*, was member of the Political Commission and responsible for MIR´s military

---

33 *Juancho* was taken by SIFA agents in the house of Eliodoro Yañez (grandson of a famous Chilean statesman by the same name), whose nickname to his friends and family was "El Cuco". Both Cuco and his wife "Cuquita" were placed in house arrest at the time of *Juancho*´s fall.

work. He was taken by SIFA in March 1974. He was shot in the stomach and stayed in a military hospital for a long time. At the beginning of July 1974, the Head of SIFA, Edgar Cevallos Jones, sent a message to Miguel Enriquez. SIFA wanted to negotiate with MIR. The terms of the negotiation offer would be made known once contact had been established. Miguel Enriquez requested Allende´s sister, Laura Allende, then a congresswoman for the Socialist Party to represent him in the meeting with SIFA. Laura Allende did so in the company of Carlos Camus, Bishop of Linares and Secretary of the Catholic Church's Bishop Conference. SIFA´s proposal was the following: MIR should cease all hostilities towards the Junta and give up all its weapons, together with handing over all information related to its political work with members of the armed forces. In return, SIFA would liberate all MIR prisoners; send all MIR members within the armed forces abroad; as well as eventually considering acceptance of MIR's presence in Chile on condition that no political opposition take place.

This proposal was a part of the power struggle taking place in the military junta which took power on the day of the coup. The members of the military junta were Pinochet, the Commander-in-Chief of the Army, Gustavo Leigh Guzmán, Commander in Chief of the Air Force, José Toribio Merino, Commander in Chief of the Navy and César Mendoza Durán, Head of the Caribineros (the Chilean police force). Leigh opposed Pinochet's growing power in the military junta. If Leigh could show that he had neutralized MIR, his position in the military junta would be considerably strengthened. Miguel demanded that Laura Allende and Bishop Camus be given the possibility of consulting with Arturo Villavela and Roberto Moreno, members of MIR's Political Commission, who both rejected the proposal. Miguel Enriquez agreed with their position, and later MIR made a public statement on the first anniversary of the coup, where the incident was exposed.[34] Cevallos was very disappointed and the torture of MIR prisoners in the AGA continued.

Another compañero who also fell into the hands of SIFA was "*Pato*" or Francisco Pizarro Meniconi. *Pato* would later become a very close family friend in Sweden. After six months at the AGA most of the political prisoners were moved to the public jail in Santiago, the "Penitenciaria de Santiago". In April 1975, thirteen members of MIR who had been imprisoned by the SIFA, including Arturo Villavela, Roberto Moreno, *Gaspar*, *Juancho* and Pato were court-martialed under military law in the Trial 84/74. This was the second court martial by the Air Force and SIFA of members of the MIR, in which they were accused of terrorism. The first trial had taken place a year earlier and involved 57 members of the armed forces that had been members of MIR. A number of them were sentenced to death. The second trial, Trial 84/74, only lasted one day. Even though there was a complete lack of evidence, all were sentenced to many years in prison. *Juancho* was sentenced to fifteen years and *Gaspar* to ten. Later, *Juancho´s*, *Gaspar´s* and *Pato´s* families would appeal for the prison sentences to be exchanged for exile under the rules of the Decree 504[35]. Most of those whose appeal was accepted were able to leave Chile under the Decree 504 in the first half of 1976. However MIR members would leave only after having received the permission to do so from MIRs political commission. Arturo Villavela left Chile in 1977. MIR considered that they could do more for the resistance struggle abroad in freedom, than if they stayed in jail for many years in Chile.

---

34 "Reply from MIR to the Gorilas", Public Declaration by MIR September 1974, "Archivo Chile", CEME

35 Concerning *Juancho* (Mario Espinosa), there was a letter written on December 9 at the Center for Nuclear research in Strasbourg, signed by 31 scientists and researchers, and sent to the Chilean Commission for Pardons, demanding that his sentence of 15 years in prison be exchanged for exile, in order for him to be able to continue his work within nuclear physics, at the Center in Strasbourg.

In the beginning of 1974, the secret services had changed their tactic. After the mass arrests that had targeted the Unidad Popular supporters, the intelligence services started focusing mainly on the MIR, but also on the Socialist and the Communist parties. The role of SIFA diminished, and DINA became the dominating intelligence force. Contreras answered directly to Pinochet. This fact also reflected the balance of power within the junta; Pinochet managed to outmaneuver the other three members of the military junta. It became increasingly clear that he was Chile´s dictator and that his power was unrestricted. Since MIR was the only party with a stated goal of undertaking and encouraging active and broad resistance, DINA intended to eradicate both the organization and its members and, above all, its leaders. At that point MIR´s resistance did not consist of armed resistance but rather anti-junta propaganda and actions of sabotage. However that did not influence the military forces´ intentions or actions. According to the Rettig investigation (2001)[36] , most of those assassinated during 1974 and 1975 were MIR members.

The most well-known MIR leaders had already been identified by military intelligence before the coup, and they were the most wanted. Dago, being MIRs most senior leader in the Santiago region, was extremely persecuted – something that I was unaware of at the time. MIR's strategy of going underground was initially successful for the most part. The changed appearances, the new way of working and the safe houses gave protection during the first period after the coup. Still some compañeros and compañeras did fall, either because they had been recognized, betrayed or because they hadn´t followed MIR´s internal security rules. One of those rules was to never ever contact a close relative and, of course, the most

---

36 "Informe de la Comisión Nacional de Verdad y Reconciliación", the official investigation known by its authors Raul Rettig et al

golden rule of all was to never give intelligence regarding anyone if you fell in the hands of the intelligence services.

Within MIR we spoke of staying firm, that is to maintain your integrity if you fell, to not break ("quebrarse"), to not betray. However, some of those *compañeros* and *compañeras* that were savagely tortured were unable to maintain complete silence, and did finally give up some, if not all, the information that the torturers wanted. Sometimes the *compañero* or *compañera* maintained their silence for a day or two in the hope that their arrest had been noted by MIR and safeguards had been taken. This worked, but not always. The rule was that if a MIR member didn´t show up for a pre-arranged meeting or didn´t return to his or her safe house in the evening, it should be assumed that they had fallen, and his/her nearest contact was to immediately leave their own safe houses and abstain from any intent to re-establish contact. Unfortunately some compañeros and compañeras trusted those that had fallen to such a degree that these basic security rules weren´t followed, and they thus committed mistakes that led to their own capture and/or death. A not uncommon tactic that DINA used was to arrest a close relative of the person they wanted to get information from; a parent, sibling or even a child; and proceeded to torture them in front of the prisoner. This method broke more than one person. With the information obtained under torture about networks and contacts, planned meetings, and the addresses of safe houses, even more *compañeros* could be taken by the intelligence forces. It became a tragic domino game.

The intelligence service sometimes managed to "turn" a *compañero* or *compañera* so that they started to collaborate with the intelligence services and actively betray members of their organizations. This happened to MIR as well as to other Left parties like the Socialist and the Communist parties. Within MIR there are some infamous examples; one of the worst was Marcia Merino, called

"Skinny Alejandra" (la "Flaca Alejandra"), who not only betrayed her closest *compañeros* and personal friends but also actively collaborated with DINA agents by accompanying them on the streets and pointing out those who she recognized. This method was called "porotear" (bean-picking) and was much used by DINA. She was eventually released and allowed to live in an apartment paid for by DINA and even given a salary. She became an active member of the intelligence services. Another form of betrayal took place when four members of MIR took part in a televised press conference, arranged by DINA, where they called on MIR to abandon the resistance struggle in February 1975.

At the beginning of February I travelled back to Peru for a brief visit. As I recall, I went back to pick up the rest of my belongings that I had left behind in Lima. When I had gone to Santiago I didn´t know how long I would be staying and only had a few things with me. When I explained to Dago that I needed to make that trip, Dago gave me an assignment: to give a message to a contact within a Peruvian left organization, which I did. In Peru I met my friend Agneta Lind who had also planned to do research in Chile, but who didn´t get further than Peru where she tried to carry out her project, but it had proved difficult. We talked in depth about the situation in Chile. I took the opportunity of writing a private letter to Tor regarding my own plans, and also sent him a report about the situation in Chile, as I understood it. I would be sending him more reports during my time in Chile. Tor kept these reports and returned them to me when I at last went back to Sweden

Both Tor and Stefan de Vylder were active in the Chile Solidarity Committee. Tor was responsible for international issues.

It can be mentioned that the Swedish Chile Solidarity Committee was set up already in 1972, as a protest against the blockade of Chilean copper exports during the Allende government. The copper mines had been nationalized by Allende and the former northamerican owners demanded that the buyers of the copper (in this case a Swedish company) not pay the Chilean government. The committee later grew fast after the coup and in the early eighties it had 86 local branches. For many years it campaigned against the Pinochet dictatorship and collected funds to help political prisoners in Chile. There were similar Solidarity Committees all over Europe.

In my private letter to Tor, I told him that I had decided to stay in Chile for maybe about six months, but that it could be longer. I told him that I had received an offers from the International Labour Organization (ILO)'s Regional Employment Programme for Latin America and the Caribbean (Programa Regional de Empleo para América Latina y el Caribe – PREALC) and the Latin American Demographic Centre (Centro Latinoamericano de Demografía – CELADE) to continue my research project with one of them. I hoped that one of the two centres would finance the processing of primary data, which my scholarship funds would not cover. I also wrote "another reason for my decision to stay in Chile is that the situation is very dynamic…I also feel quite identified with Chile by now…your prediction about where my sympathies would lie – do you recall our discussion at the African restaurant in Paris late one night? – was very accurate". I was of course referring to MIR. I ended the letter "I am at present studying intensely a time series analysis so that I won´t appear completely ignorant" once I start working at one of the institutes. "Apart from that everything is quite calm". This letter was written on January 23, 1974; the last sentence was probably meant to reassure Tor and my other Swedish friends.

The report that I sent a few days later to Tor had a different tone:

1. *Military power: The oppression and persecution continue unabated in Chile five months after the coup. It's no longer about merely arresting people who sympathized with the Unidad Popular but, above all, those who were active members in the parties in Unidad Popular, including union leaders. MIR members are being particularly targeted. The difference from the initial period after the coup, is that now the military know exactly who they are looking for, and the persecution is more specific and concentrated. The military kidnap wives and children of active members and hold them as hostages in order to capture the militants (without any great success)....In the north of Chile in the former saltpeter mines there are two concentration camps for political prisoners, in which it is estimated that there are over 7000 prisoners. Many of those who were arrested in the first months after the coup, and have been judged as less important, have been released. But people who publicly criticize the military are still being arrested and tortured to force them to confess that they have offended the military and therefor also have offended the Chilean Fatherland ("la Patria Chilena). It is obvious that the military don´t have the situation under control. There are often military patrols on the streets. In strategic places in Santiago, you can see three or four soldiers with machine-guns behind sandbags and shooting is heard every night. The soldiers are very alert and very tense. The military have declared that power will not be rotated among the four leaders of the junta, and it is obvious that the junta is divided.*

2. *The general resistance: it´s hard to report on concrete events since almost everything we hear is in the form of unconfirmed rumors so I can only report my own observations. Some months back the fear of reprisals was so great among the general public that comments on the situation were only made among very close friends. On buses and on the street you wouldn´t hear*

anyone comment aloud on the situation, except for the "momios" (mummies, slang term for reactionaries). Today the situation is different- in public places you can hear angry comments on the high prices, on the continued house searches and harassment. The expression "the military have gone too far" ("los milicos se pasaron") is very common. The resistance grows steadily, even among those who formerly were against Unidad Popular. There are more people against the military than those that supported Unidad Popular and most of the Christian Democrats are very critical. 37 The period after the coup has been characterized by growing consciousness and militancy among the working class. This is a result of the continued oppression as well as the deteri- orating situation for the working class in particular. Spontaneous resistance actions occur frequently, for example mutiny in the regiments and bomb attacks against military installations.

3. *The economy: The rate of inflation has gone up to 500% after the coup. Only this January prices doubled for many products and are prices are now far higher in the black-market than be- fore the coup. The prices on food products have been liberal- ized, and one example is the price for food oil which now costs 900 escudos while sugar costs 300 escudos. The normal daily wage is between 300-400 escudos. Transport prices have risen as well: a worker who takes two buses back and forth to work every day has to pay 3000 escudos every month just on trans- port. Officially the minimum wage is 18 000 escudos per month, but the majority of the working class do not get more than 10 -12 000 escudos. This means that even those with a job have a difficult time surviving. There is a risk of outright hunger for many people. According to the junta, unemployment is 15%, but*

---

37 The Christian Democrats initially supported the military coup, my comment at the time of writing

it is safe to assume that the real number is much higher. Prices are expected to go up further. Small shopkeepers have started hoarding and queues are often long. Since prices are so high, the real market is very small and only the upper classes can afford to buy what they need. There is wide-spread dissatisfaction among small business owners. The junta has also decided to do away with tariffs on imported goods which means that those that produce for the domestic market now have to compete with cheaper imported goods. The junta wants to promote the export industry which reflects their alliance with the national and international bourgeoisie, to the detriment of the domestic small bourgeoisie and the working class. This is also one of the reasons behind the widespread dissatisfaction with and resistance towards the junta. Credits have been given from the imperialist countries but often with very short repayment terms. Foreign investments are taking place, in particular from Brazil. The land that had been expropriated has been returned to its former owners, as well as many of those industries that were nationalized during Allende.

4. *The political situation: All political parties as well as the Central Union of Workers (Central Unitaria de Trabajadores – CUT) have been banned and there is no sign that the junta will allow any form of political activity. Some unions, like the metalworkers' union, are still functioning but underground. It is obvious that the class contradictions have intensified and that the only way for the junta to stay in power is to continue with, and increase, its oppression of those who oppose it. The Unidad Popular parties have been more or less crushed and have great difficulties in re-organizing. In contrast MIR, that had foreseen the coup and prepared itself for it, managed to keep its organization intact and is now working efficiently underground. At ground level within all the important sectors there are activities taking place, often in a*

joint nucleus of MIR, Communist Party and Socialist Party members. The Communist Party at leadership level doesn´t want to collaborate with MIR but at ground level it is different and occurs frequently. There is cause for optimism and the armed struggle is being prepared, slowly but surely.

At the end of the letter, I write: *This is the first report. Please confirm that you have received it by referring to the date (February 5). The next letters will be in English[38] and will be signed Margaret.*

After a week in Peru, I returned to Chile.

Before I moved into my new apartment on the Avenida Santa Maria close to the Bellavista neighborhood I was still living in Tom´s house. While I was there, I had the opportunity of meeting Tom´s close friends from ECLA and even the few remaining Swedes. Among them were Lilian Indseth and Sonia Martinsson who were both working as local employees at the Swedish Embassy. I also met an older Swedish lady, Susanne Aurelius, who had earlier also worked at ECLA. Susanne would subsequently help me to get a job at ECLA as a locally employed researcher, which proved very beneficial for my façade. I also met four Germans, slightly older than me, who worked at different UN institutions in Santiago: Rolf, Stephanie[39], Dieter and his wife. They had studied in Heidelberg and knew each other from that time and were Left sympathizers. I became good friends with these Germans, particularly with Stephanie who came to play an important role during my time in Chile. I soon understood that they were also engaged in helping people who were at risk, but we avoided talking about this in order to not share sensitive information unnecessarily. I had the impression that it was the Socialist

---

38 This first letter was in Swedish
39 Stephanie is not her real name

party that was their primary contact. In order to dimmish the tension that we lived under, we tried to have some normal activities like car outings to the nearby countryside.

In particular I remember a visit that we made to a farm that was owned by a German family. We had been invited and were taken around the extensive holdings with vineyards, and later invited to a barbecue. Everything was very pleasant until we discovered something that almost made us choke. It became clear that the head of the family was an old Nazi who had managed to escape to Chile after the Second World War, a past he was very proud of and for which he had no regrets. We had to keep straight faces and not reveal the shock we experienced. It was obvious that you could never know, when meeting new acquaintances, what side they were on. The upper class were for the most part "mummies" and hated people from the Left. The risks were therefore high if you were unable to conceal your feelings at social encounters like these. Needless to say, that was the last of our outings. From then on, the encounters between myself and my German friends were scarcer and took place with more measures of security. I could naturally never invite them to my apartment in Santa Maria or anywhere else that I lived, since my address needed to be kept secret.

Resistance in practice

In the beginning of 1974, Dago and I drove around in his car, and we had time to talk a lot in between his meetings. I wanted to learn more about MIR´s politics and why MIR had stayed outside the UP; what the goals of the resistance movement were; how MIR judged the conditions for actively and successfully carrying out the resistance; how MIR judged the capacity of the military to continue with the oppression, particularly against the background of the enormous support that the Left had during the Allende government, plus many other issues. Dago explained patiently. This was something that came naturally to him and revealed his natural leadership qualities. He talked enthusiastically about MIR: about MIR´s analysis and considerations regarding political developments; about MIR´s view on the situation of different countries in Latin America and globally. At that time, I didn´t know what his position within MIR was but it was clear that he had a key role and that the compañeros who got in the car had an enormous respect for him. They took his instructions without questioning. Gradually a deep trust grew between us. Dago started to share internal MIR documents for me to read as well as the MIR newsletter "El Rebelde" (The Rebel), all of them in miniature format. I had to get a strong magnifying glass in order to read them!

"El Rebelde" began to be published during the FREI regime (1964-1970). It continued to be published during the UP government, first as a monthly and later as a bi-weekly newsletter analyzing current political processes, as well as being a mouthpiece for MIR´s political line. After the coup, El Rebelde began to play an important role in building the resistance movement. Its political analysis contributed to an understanding of the military dictatorship´s long-term ambitions and it became a key communications vehicle for the resistance. It tried to inspire and to instruct regarding different forms of resistance, and how they could be organized and carried out. Examples of this were how to create small "Comités de Resistencia"(resistance committees) in the workplace; neighborhoods; the shanty town areas; high schools and universities. The committees could be organized with between 3 – 7 people, they could print and spread propaganda against the military; support sabotage actions, boycotts, go slows or strikes; hunger strikes and other forms of protest. El Rebelde addressed itself broadly to all those who opposed the dictatorship but particularly of course to the Left and to the unions. Later on, it would also address the human rights groups that were created, such as the groups of relatives of political prisoners and the disappeared. In order to avoid detection El Rebelde was distributed in hard paper copy in miniature or as microfilm.[40]

I wondered how the resistance was supposed to function in practical terms, and while visiting the library at the British Institute in

40 From "El relato de la prensa mirista durante la dictadura civico-militar 1973-1989" by Robinson Silva Hidalgo

Santiago, I found some books about the resistance movements in Europe during the Second World War. I read them with great interest. The stories regarding the French resistance movement were of special interest; they explained how contacts and communication were managed; hiding places and information gathering were described, and so on. The context in Chile was of course completely different but still there were valuable lessons to be learned regarding security measures. I remember particularly a trick on how to create one´s own security network. If one needed help or support, one should never turn to anyone that was a close friend or relative, or to anyone who was close to or relative of someone who had fallen. Instead, one could turn to people who were known to and trusted by, but still outside, these immediate circles. It may seem obvious, but it became a golden rule for me. "El Nancho", Hernan Aguiló, a compañero within MIR, would become someone with whom I had close contact for a period, and he followed this rule rigorously.

Another matter related to security rules was that we needed to be constantly vigilant regarding what went on around us. For example, we knew which vehicles the DINA agents used and we went on alert when we spotted one of them. Initially the DINA agents used cars of the mark Opel, and pick-up trucks type C 10 of the mark Chevrolet that had been requisitioned from the former government services. When we saw these vehicles we had to immediately take another route, or if on foot, immediately enter a nearby store or buildning. Another characteristic was that often several DINA agents, often four at a time, travelled together in the cars. Otra característica de la DINA es que andaban varios hombres juntos en los autos, muchas veces cuatro a la vez. This was a signal for us to go on high alert.

When I moved into my one-bedroom apartment on the Avenida Santa Maria, I had obtained, at Dago´s request, a powerful short-wave radio. I could listen to news services, like the BBC in London,which broadcasted international news from the rest of the world. The lack of news from the outside world was very frustrating for MIR, and this led to a new assignment for me. Dago asked me to listen to the news every evening and to write down a short summary on a page, or half a page, every day. Dago came to my apartment several times a week and I would hand over my news coverage. Dago continued to use my apartment for longer meetings than those that he normally held in the car. He would read my news reports on these occasions. He let me know that he liked my way of summarizing events and that he was impressed by them. When he held his meetings, I would prepare some food for us to eat. This served the purpose of staying out of the way during the meetings and also making sure Dago and his meeting partner had something to eat, which was not always a priority for them. Sometimes, when he had spare time between meetings, Dago would come alone, in order not to have to spend time unnecessarily on the street. By then it was obvious that we were attracted to one another. One thing led to another, and we wound up starting a relationship. Dago had been completely open from the start that he had a fiancée, who had also been active in MIR, during the last few years. She had, however, sought asylum at an embassy in December 73. Dago was also clear about the fact that it wasn´t likely that they would meet again, at least not for many years. That knowledge pained him, but he was determined to live in the present.

The physical proximity was welcome. During brief breaks in the privacy of my apartment we were able to give each other love and tenderness. It can´t be denied that the very abnormal reality that we lived in was dominated by constant nervous tension and often fear. Outside the apartment, on the street, we were obliged to be permanently alert and attentive to our surroundings, to unknown people and events in our proximity, and to constantly analyze possible risks and signs that could indicate that we were under observation or being followed. Lack of attention to details could be the difference between life and death. In that situation our relationship was an indescribable comfort and solace for both of us. It provided us with a brief escape from the harsh reality outside. The intimacy between us also permitted Dago to relax his normally quite hard exterior and share personal aspects of his life like his family and his childhood and his time as a student. In those moments he was a loving, warm, and tender man. Naturally he was very careful not to reveal details, but I did learn about his enormous respect for his mother, a teacher, and a very intelligent woman. I learnt that he came from a large family in the south of Chile, that he had both brothers and sisters, and that he was the oldest of all the siblings. Being the oldest had probably contributed to his natural authority. Dago often talked about the discrimination that he had witnessed in the rural areas where he grew up, and how poor farmers suffered injustices. We talked about the future and of a vision of Chile as a free country once again, where people could live well and where everyone´s rights would be respected. We also talked about more trivial things, like what music we liked, and who were our favorite authors. When he saw that I was reading "Rayuela" by Julio Cortazar he became very enthusiastic, Cortazar was one of his favorites. We talked about all kinds of different things, and it helped us both to relax momentarily.

Now that I had moved into my apartment I needed to work on my façade, as a research student at one of Santiago´s many international institutes. What originally had started out as the purpose of my stay in Chile, to gather material for my thesis in economic history, had now become a façade. This was so because the military had closed the universities and the public archives, so it was actually impossible to conduct research. After having received the notice from FLACSO that I couldn´t be there, I reached out to the head of the Latin America Demographic Centre (Centro Latinoamericano de Demografía – CE-LADE), Carmen Miró. She was from Panama and was considered the foremost Latin American demographer at that time. She was very considerate and welcoming, and offered me a workplace at the institute. This had the added advantage of being close to where I lived and so I could walk there, which was also very positive as I could go home for lunch and have Dago over (mostly for his meetings). If the neighbors saw us they would take us for a young couple in a romantic relationship – which wasn´t completely wrong.

Once at CELADE it was a little difficult to maintain the pretense, but most people didn´t ask me very much about what I was doing. I did spend quite a lot of time going through what statistics were available within my area. At times other people from nearby institutes would come over for "after work" socializing. One of them was Fernando Enrique Cardoso who worked at the Latin American Institute for Economic and Social Planning (Instituto Latinoamericano de Planificación Económica y Social – ILPES) at the time. Later he would become president of Brazil. We played chess once – I was better at chess then than now!

In April I was able to send a report to my friends in Sweden with someone who travelling abroad.

Dear friends,

I know that I haven´t written you for some time but I am sure that you understand the quite obvious difficulties in communication….it would be really fine if you could let me know as rapidly as possible whether you have written or not. It may be necessary to take further steps in security matters. When you reply I will let you know immediately.

The situation here is daily becoming worse, even though one might think that hardly was possible. Sometimes I have the impression that you have more information (in Sweden) than I have (in Chile), but in any case, I will give you some news of the latest happenings. About three weeks ago the military staged a new wave of repression while Pinochet was negotiating with his brother fascists in Brazil. It started over a weekend and continued for about a week. That weekend, four of the top leaders of the Socialist Party were captured. Among them were the "Pollo Rus", secretary general of their PS central committee here. Also, around 150 militants from the base level from this and other parties were arrested. We believe that the success in the military raid was largely due to faulty security in the Socialist Party.

For about a week, soldiers stopped public buses all over the capital, forcing people to get off and show identification. Many were taken away for "interrogation". Whole blocks in the center of Santiago were roped off and everybody within its limits were forced to undergo the same process just mentioned. On the Sunday of this particular weekend, an entire "población" (roughly= slum area) was encircled by soldiers at 05:30 in the morning, the end of the "toque de queda" for that night, and house searches of every single house in the area were carried out. Every male over 15 years of age was taken away to a football field, where they were held prisoners while the soldiers interrogated them one by one. There were around five thousand men, mostly workers, unemployed and some students. The number of men who after this were definitely arrested and taken away is unknown. The official explanation was that these drastic measures were taken to catch delinquents and criminals. This is a familiar story by now.

I am sure that you know of the death, after torture, of General Bachelet, who was a constitutionalist Air Force general who opposed the coup, and of the murder of José Tohá[41], minister under Allende, in the Military Hospital in Santiago. It may not have been a direct assassination of the latter but when a person dies of malnutrition in a military hospital here, there can be no doubt as to who is to blame. According to eyewitnesses, thousands of people followed the casket at the funeral. The words "Salvador Allende, presente!"; José Toha, presente!" were uttered and during the procession "The Internationale"[42] and "Venceremos"[43] were sung , although quickly silenced by the furious military. Needless to say, hundreds of people were arrested. It is to be feared that Clodomiro Almeyda will suffer the same fate as Toha, being held prisoner in the School of Tele-communications in Santiago and gravely undernourished. His wife is allowed to see him but not to bring him food or blankets.

I believe I mentioned the growing opposition to the junta among the Christian Democrats in my last letter. Since then, the fact that the director of the television channel 13 (operated by the CD) and the president of the law school at the Universidad de Chile, as well as 18 top advisers and members of staff of the government administration, all CD, have all been fired from their jobs and Frei "on vacation" in Argentina, definitely does not point to any improvement in the relationship between the junta and the Christian Democrat Party.

On a more general level, it can be said that the military are increasing their repression using all kinds of intelligence services,

---

41 José Tohá was Minister of the Interior and National Defense in Allende´s government
42 "The Internationale" is an international anthem and has been the standard of socialist movements since the mid-nineteenth century.
43 "Venceremos"or "We Will Overcome", the anthem for Allende's Unidad Popular during their successful presidential campaign and government.

to attempt to smoke out militants underground. Depressingly enough, most of the parties of the UP are totally uncoordinated at party level and are not functioning. The exception to this is the party I emphasized in my last letter (*MIR) whose central committee and political commission is intact with the exception of one member, and where a relatively small percentage of its militants at base level have been caught. Among the masses there can be no doubt that the opposition continues. Sabotage in factories is extremely common. Workers deliberately slow down their speed of working and worsen the quality of their products. At the same time the situation of the working class is disastrous. We calculate an inflation of 1000% since the first of January 1973, with a raise in wages of only 500% in the same period. Begging and digging in garbage cans for food was seldom seen before but is now not uncommon.

There is much to be done and those who are doing it are extremely busy. If the necessary precautions are taken the dangers are not that great. The consequences are known to everyone and it is a hard fact that must be learned to be lived with, otherwise everything would grind to a halt. And it is simply not possible to convince a starving worker or peasant that he must stoically accept the resent situation. On the contrary, he will tell you : "we have blood in our eye, we feel hate, and one day we shall get our own back. It is only a matter of time".

As for me, please do not worry. I really am being extremely careful. Outwardly it may seem that nothing is happening, but the foundations are slowly being laid for a great change. I am profoundly satisfied and proud of being a part of that.

All my love,
Margareth

Time passed and all of a sudden, at the end of March, Dago stopped getting in touch and stopped coming by. My first thought was that he had fallen. His silence and absence were extremely alarming. After a couple of weeks, I decided to try to somehow get in touch with MIR and find out what had happened. The question was how. I had no alternative contacts. After a lot of thought I reached out to Sonia at the Swedish Embassy. I knew that she was responsible for the Cuban residence, and that Max Marambio (*"Joel"*) was there waiting to leave the country.

Max had at one point been a MIR member and also part of GAP ("Grupo de Amigos del Presidente"), the unit that had been President Allende´s personal security guard. The GAP had been created in 1970 through a request that Allende made directly to Miguel Enriquez, since the Socialist Party to which Allende belonged lacked people with the necessary training. So, when the GAP was created, it consisted of MIR members. Later, when MIR broke with Allende, this changed, and the task was assumed by the Socialist Party. The break between Allende and MIR happened as a consequence of the assassination by the police (Carabineros), of Moisés Huentelaf, at the end of 1971. Huentelaf was from the Mapuche nation, a *campesino*[44] leader of MIR's organization of rural workers, the Revolutionary Campesino Movement (Movimiento de Campesinos Revolucionarios – MCR) in the south of Chile.

I suspected that Max, who was in the Cuban residence and whom Dago had told me about, and who still had direct contact with MIR´s General Secretary Miguel Enriquez even from within the Cuban

---

[44] "Campesinos" and "campesinas" are rural producers, who work small- and medium- sized plots, with the family constituting most or all of the labor. It is sometimes translated as "peasant" in English, but it's meaning is broader, covering small- and medium- size farmers, landless people, women farmers, indigenous people, migrants and agricultural workers.

residence, was someone that I could turn to even if we didn´t know one another. Many years later I would meet Max on a number of occasions. Max had made sure that all the weapons that the Cubans had left, planned for self-defense use in emergency circumstances, if the embassy were to be attacked by the military, were eventually smuggled out and turned over to MIR. The weapons were taken out hidden in empty gas cannisters. In Chile at the time gas was used for domestic cooking and heating, so it was common to exchange empty gas cannisters for filled ones and in that way the cannisters were ideal camouflage for transporting the weapons. After some time Max was given free passage and was able to leave Chile in July 1974.[45] Many years later I would meet Max on various occasions.

I wrote a brief letter to Miguel signed Isabel, where I told him about my work together with *Diego* (Dago´s political name at the time), and the date when our contact had been broken. I explained that I was fine but worried about the loss of contact and requested instructions. I wrote my letter on cigarette paper, hid it in a small package, and gave it to Sonia who was kind enough to pass it on to Max. I had to give Sonia an explanation, but I never had to regret doing so. It took some time before I received a reply, which consisted of instructions. I was to walk on a street close to my workplace on a certain day, at a certain hour, with a certain women´s magazine sticking out from my purse in a visible way. If someone approached me and asked me what time it was, I was to answer a time which was half an hour later. If no one approached me, I was to repeat the procedure a few days later. This was the recognition method ("santo y seña") that was used in the resistance to establish contact between two people who didn´t know each other. In effect no one approached me the first time I did it, only on the second attempt did we establish contact. The reason behind this slightly complicated

---

45 See "Las armas de ayer" by Max Marambio

procedure was later explained to me; the first time I did it no one approached me because I was being watched by MIR compañeros to see if anyone from the intelligence services was following me or had me under surveillance. It was important to follow this procedure to avoid possible traps. Once it was established that everything was ok, the contact could be made. Contacts were mostly only established on a second or third occasion, once it was determined to be safe.

What had happened was that a female compañera, who had come to my apartment with Dago on one occasion, had fallen. It had been determined that she had given up some information and it was feared that my address might have been one of those things, in which case I would already have fallen as well. So, for security reasons Dago had broken the contact with me until the situation could be cleared up. Much later I realized that this type of situation – being cut off or disconnected ("desconectado/a") – occurred very often for very many people. Ideally there was always supposed to be alternative ways of re-establishing contact but if they didn´t exist you had to use your own astuteness without endangering other compañeros.

My contact on that particular day turned out to be Lumi Videla, nick-named "La Negra". She was a beautiful and charming young woman. She gave me the following instructions: to abandon my present apartment and rent a new apartment as soon as possible and to move immediately. I was not to share my new address with anyone. She gave me money and a couple of weeks to arrange the matter. We agreed a time to meet again. The apartment should be relatively modest and located in the middle-class area close to the Providencia avenue. As luck would have it I was able to arrange this quite rapidly in accordance with the specifications. Only after I had moved into the new place did I see Dago again.

Lumi Videla

More or less at the same time that this happened, I changed jobs. My friend, Susanne Aurelius, had informed me that ECLA needed to present a paper at the first global women´s conference the following year. It was called the United Nations World Conference of the International Women´s Year and took place in Mexico in 1975. ECLA wanted to employ someone who could write about women´s economic situation in Latin America and have the paper ready in time for the conference. Susanne, who knew of my academic background, recommended me and I was hired as a locally employed research assistant. This was a great step forward in my façade because for the first time I had a solid legitimate reason to be in Chile.

In May, soon after I had moved into my new apartment right off Seminario street and had been able to see Dago again, he asked me if he could use my place as safe house for a compañero who had to leave Santiago soon. The new apartment was smaller in size than my former one, but it was more practical since it had two bedrooms, which was an advantage. Where this compañero was going or who he was, I wasn´t told. I just knew that some logistical issues had to be solved before he could leave the city. The compañero who came, and stayed for three weeks, was Alejandro Villalobos.

Alejandro didn´t have any qualms about volunteering his real name although I didn´t ask, of course. He was known politically as "*Comandante Mickey*", and he was a well-known leader from the Movement of Revolutionary Shanty Town Dwellers (Movimiento de Pobladores Revolucionarios – MPR) in the enormous shanty town Nueva La Habana (New Havana). After the coup the military renamed it Nuevo Amanecer (New Dawn). Alejandro was, after Victor Toro, the most persecuted leader from the shanty town dwellers' movement. Much later I learned that Lumi Videla had worked close to *Mickey* in Nueva La Habana and together with others they had carried out extraordinary and committed social work there, such as setting up schools for children who had never had a chance to go to school, with the poor during the Allende government. Thanks to *Mickey* and Lumi among others, Nueva La Habana became, in many ways, a model society among the shanty towns.[46] *Mickey* was a very sympathetic person who was very easy to get to know. It was quite pleasant to have him as a house guest for a few weeks. Of course, he could never go out and in practical terms I was his "palo blanco" or caretaker.

From *Mickey* I learnt a lot about the living conditions in the shanty towns, and how deep the poverty there was. *Mickey* left for Valparaiso, where he was not as well-known as in Santiago, after he left my apartment.
Some weeks after he had left I unexpectedly received a letter from

---

[46] This is information provided by Lumi´s brother Lautaro Videla Moya known as "Chico Santiago", available in a documentary film on Lumi produced by the Universidad Academia de Humanismo Cristiano.

him that moved me deeply. I quote it in Spanish, the translation is found below.

Alejandro Villalobos, el "Comandante Mickey"

Querida camarada Isabel

Camarada, la (he) extrañado mucho, me había acostumbrado mucho contigo…estoy seguro que algún día volveremos a vernos. Creo haber tenido mucha suerte al conocer una compañera como tú, dispuesta a entregar la vida por los pobres y explotados de este país, porque en ti se encarna el internacionalismo proletario. Los pobres, los explotados y los revolucionarios nos sentimos orgullosos de tener en nuestras filas una persona como tú, que no tienes miedo de entregar hasta la última gota de su sangre por la liberación de los humildes del mundo. Compañera te repito tu eres ejemplo del internacionalismo proletario, yo no creía mucho pero tú me enseñaste que existe….camarada cuídese mucho porque revolucionarias como tu necesitamos mucho para la victoria final. Isabel este es a lo mejor el ultimo papel que te escribe pero quiero que sepas que te respeto y te admiro mucho…siempre te recordare´ como una gran revoluciona-ria….te abraza tu camarada de lucha. Mil veces morir de pie que vivir de rodillas!! Patria o muerte, venceremos! Hasta la victoria siempre!

Translation:

Dear compañera Isabel: Compañera, I have missed you a lot, I had become accustomed to living at your place and being with you …I am sure we will meet again. I believe that I was very lucky to get to know a compañera like you, who is pre-pared to give her life for the poor and the oppressed in this country. You are the incarnation of proletarian internation-alism. We, the poor, the oppressed and the revolutionaries, are proud to have a person like yourself among us, who isn´t afraid to spill her last drop of blood for the liberation of the humble of this earth. Compañera, I repeat, you are an exam-ple of proletarian internationalism. I didn´t believe very much in it before, but you have taught me that it really exists…..com-pañera, take great care because we need revolutionaries like yourself, in order to reach the final victory. Isabel maybe this is the last letter that I will be able to write to you, but I want you to know that I respect you and admire you a lot…I will always remember you as a great revolutionary …your comrade in arms embraces you. A thousand times better to die on your feet than to live on your knees! Fatherland or death, we will triumph! Until victory, always!
The letter made me cry but it also strengthened my determination, and my belief that what I was doing was right.

We never met again. *Mickey* finally fell on January 19, 1975, when he was shot to death by the intelligence services. He had decided not to be taken alive. *Mickey* was 29 years when he was killed.

Quite soon after I had moved into my apartment by Seminario, Dago brought me internal documents to read. The more I read, the more I was convinced that MIR´s analysis of the situation and the strategic direction it charted, were correct. I should mention that I had explained to Dago that if I was to work for the Resistance, I wanted to be a member of MIR. He explained to me that there were three steps. The first step was to work as a sympathizer – which was more or less what I was doing already. The next step was to become a candidate ("aspirante"), which required being able to carry out more advanced tasks, as well as showing a good understanding of MIR´s policies and capacity to implement them. As a candidate you were applying for full membership. After some time, it was possible to become a combatant ("militante") or full member, through being accepted as such by either the Secretary General – Miguel – or another member of the Political Commission. So as part of this process I was allowed to study internal documents that focused on analysis of the situation and decisions regarding the Resistance struggle. Ironically one of the documents that Dago gave me contained information that he himself had been elected to integrate the Political Commission. The document gave a full explanation of his background and the responsibilities that he had held in MIR up to that point. It was through that explanation, where it mentioned for example that he had been a student of sociology, that I was able to understand that Diego – as I called him – was Dagoberto Perez Vargas. I had to tell him that I had guessed his true identity, based on the details that he had shared regarding his youth and his background. Dago was unhappy when he understood that I had discovered his identity, but there was nothing that could be done about it at that point.

After *Mickey* left, I stayed on in the apartment for some time. However, Dago considered that it had security issues. If I remember correctly this was due to the fact that the apartment was located on a small street that was a blind alley. This would be a huge drawback if it was necessary to escape rapidly and, due to my inexperience, I hadn't been aware of that problem. Dago decided that it would be better to get a new place. He also wanted me to buy a car since it was safer to drive in one´s own car than to use the public transport. Since I had started working at ECLA it was relatively easy to find a house to rent. This time it was a small house with several exits. I was also able to buy a car, a turquoise Fiat.

The move to the house was planned to take place at the end of August but exactly at that time I became very ill. It turned out that I had caught hepatitis. I was ordered by a doctor, who had been recommended by my friend Stephanie, to stay in bed for at least 14 days with medication. The hepatitis was probably a result of my indulgence in fresh seafood which I used to buy at the central market in Santiago. This doctor became extremely worried about me when he received my laboratory blood tests, and he even came to visit me at my house to check on me. Even though I was extremely weak, I managed with great effort to carry out the move from my apartment to the new house. Fortunately, I didn´t have so many things to move! I remember that I had a high fever and could only drive with difficulty. The new house was located on the Calle Bustos close to Plaza Uruguay and with the help of Anita (Tom´s former housekeeper) I was able to get installed. Anita stayed with me and made sure that I was well taken care of. I had to inform Dago that I was ill without worrying him, since to say that you were ill was often used as a code for saying that you had fallen. Finally, Dago understood that I was truly ill but safe and he still stayed away for a few weeks. When I was better, I was given new tasks. The first of these was to let Dago´s father stay at the house; Dago´s father was of course also persecuted and was on his way to enter an embassy and apply for political asylum. Dago´s father had become involuntarily separated from his wife and Dago´s youngest sister Patricia, who at that time was only 12, and they had found refuge in another place. Dago´s father was very quiet and obviously extremely unhappy. He didn´t stay for long, maybe a week. A few years later he was able to reunite with his wife and daughter in Cuba.

In the house we also had other activities. Small meetings with at the most two or three participants were held just like in my apartment in Santa Maria. The advantage was that Dago could do that even when I was at work since Anita was in the house. Anita was a very brave woman and discreet as well. She understood what we were up to but never asked any questions. There were also practical issues to taken care of. One of these was the Cuban weapons that constantly needed to be moved. Alejandro de la Barra, nicknamed "el Nano" and his wife Ana-María Puga, who were two compañeros from MIR who worked closely with Dago, and I, managed to transport many heavy Kalashnikovs and AK-47s in my car. These weapons were mostly a nuisance. Apart from the most persecuted of the MIR members, who had one or two of them for self-defense purposes, the rest of the arsenal was mostly a source of irritation since they were difficult to hide and often had to be moved to safer storage. Most MIR members had guns, which were more useful in case of a confrontation with the military.

Alejandro de la Barra was a naturally good-natured person and loved to joke. Sometimes it was hard to think that he was in fact serious revolutionary. He used to joke with me and say that I was MIR´s very own Patricia Hearst. She was the daughter of an American millionaire in the US, who had been kidnapped by the Symbiotic Liberation Army (SLA) in California in 1974. She turned around and become a member of the group. Among her activities was the participation in bank robberies that were carried out by the SLA. Ana María, Alejandro´s wife, was also extremely charming. They had a little son who attended a normal kindergarten, and, to their neighbors, they appeared to be a normal middle-class couple. The compañeros in MIR often showed an incredible sense of humor (even Dago) and could often make jokes non-stop. Dago for example would joke that Miguel still thought that I was a CIA-agent. I didn´t really appreciate that particular joke but the joking was a way to handle the harsh realities that we were dealing with.

The noose tightens

DINA´s focused persecution of MIR kept us painfully aware of the dangers all around us. More and more *compañeros* and *compañeras* were being arrested and killed during 1974. Many of them were "disappeared", and their bodies were never recovered. One of the disappeared was *Juancho´s* younger brother, Jorge Espinosa. Jorge was arrested by DINA on June 18, 1974 and taken to the torture center on 38 Londres Street.

Testimonies exist of how he was tortured, and then disappeared. He was 24 years old. DINA wanted information from him on the whereabouts of his older brother *Juancho*. Jorge kept silent and died as a consequence. Dago´s two younger brothers, who both belonged to MIR, were also arrested by DINA: Carlos, who was 25 years old at the time of his arrest and Aldo who was 3 when he was arrested. Both were killed by DINA. Some years later Dago´s younger twin siblings, Mireya and Ivan, who were also MIR members, were killed by DINA in a shoot-out. They were 21 years old at the time. Many others in MIR met the same fate but Dago´s family was a specific target. The killing of the twins, Mireya and Ivan, was a pure act of revenge.

By mid-1974, 40% of MIRs Central Committee had either been arrested or killed.

Lumi Videla, who had been my contact a few months earlier, was one of MIR´s most important woman leaders and a member of MIR´s Central Committee. She was taken by DINA on 21 September 1974. Her husband "Chico" Sergio Perez who was a member of MIR´s Political Commission, was arrested the following day. Lumi had been pointed out by the traitor la "Flaca Alejandra"(Skinny Alexandra), who had been her very close friend. Both Lumi and Chico were taken by DINA to the torture center at José Domingo Cañas 1367. Both were subjected to cruel torture and finally died as a result of it. Chico died first, on October 4th, and Lumi died a month later. Lumi´s body was thrown over the wall into the garden of the Italian Embassy on the November 4th on the direct order of Manuel Contreras. In the newspapers it said that she had been murdered inside the Italian Embassy grounds by other asylum seekers. The body of Chico Sergio was never found. The couple had been married since 1966 and had a small son. This bizarre incident with Lumi´s body became known all over the world and led to Italy severing diplomatic relations with Chile. Lumi was 26 years old and Chico 31 years old when they were killed.

A short time after Dago´s father left my house I received a new house guest. He was José Hernan Carrasco and his political name was *Marco Antonio*.

He belonged to what was called "the Central Force" and was very persecuted; he lacked a safe house at that point and so my house became his safe house for a few weeks. Later he would do something that caused consternation and disgust, but when I knew him, I just regarded him as a pleasant and easy-going comrade.

I remember asking Dago if it was possible for us to live together. I missed him very much when I didn´t see him, and his visits were always brief. He avoided answering me but later he told me that the real reason was that Miguel was against it. I never met Miguel, but it was clear that, as MIR's leader, his decisions were not to be questioned. His firm opinion was that being a foreigner, and a blond Swede at that, I was far too visible and easy to identify. In other words, Miguel regarded me as a potential security risk.

So I continued my work at ECLA and Anita continued to take care of our various house guests. I remember it as a more than a little schizophrenic; daytime I was an international public servant at a UN institute, and the rest of the time I was an active member of the Resistance movement.

On October 5th a fatal event took place. DINA discovered Miguel Enriquez's safe house on Santa Fe Street in San Miguel, a lower middle-class/working class neighborhood in Santiago. The house was surrounded by agents from DINA. The attack was led by Miguel Krasnoff Marchenko at the head of DINA´s Caupolican Brigade, which had as a mission to especially target MIR. When they arrived the DINA agents launched a grenade attack against the house. In the house, apart from Miguel, there were also other people: Carmen Castillo, Miguel´s compañera who was heavily pregnant; José Bordaz Paz known as *Coño Molina*, a member of MIR´s Central Committee and "Tito", Humberto Sotomayor from MIR´s Political Commission.

MIR´s internal rules stated that, in case of an attack, the first action was to try to repel the attack, and then to retreat. Another rule was that MIR's internal hierarchy should be respected in the retreat. This meant that, in this case, Miguel should have been the first to retreat. What happened was that Miguel was injured and tried to protect Carmen who had been hit by a hand grenade. Coño Molina and Tito Sotomayor, believing that Miguel had been killed, then fled. In fact Miguel kept firing his weapon but was finally shot to death. Miguel was 31 years old and had been MIR´s General Secretary since 1967. Carmen was arrested and taken to a hospital but ultimately lost the baby after its birth. Her life was only saved because the Vatican contacted Pinochet directly and demanded that she be released.[47]

---

47 This information was shared by Gaspar, in a conversation that we had in June 2022

Carmen´s father had been the Vice-Chancellor of the Catholic University in Santiago and was a very respected man in Chile, which meant that he had many contacts including the Vatican. He used these as soon as he found out that Carmen had been arrested. After having been interrogated in the hospital by Krasnoff, she was expelled from the country and flown abroad.

The attack against MIR´s highest leader and his death became triumphant first page news in the reactionary media in Chile. They announced that MIR had finally been crushed. The right celebrated.

The loss of Miguel was a fatal blow. It was incomprehensible to us. Many within the Left, both in Chile and abroad, considered that his leadership was irreplaceable. It was truly difficult to understand and yet more difficult to accept, and many in MIR were deeply shocked. It was a huge moral and strategic loss. Even so,there was a certain degree of preparedness in MIR as the possibility of this happening had been considered within the leadership. Andres Pascal Allende, the nephew of president Allende and member of MIR's Political Commission, assumed the leadership of the party.

Humberto Sotomayor sought asylum at a European embassy the following day together with his wife. He was immediately expelled from MIR, firstly because he had fled while Miguel was still alive and secondly because he had sought asylum. *Coño Molina* who also fled, informed MIR that Humberto Sotomayor had claimed that Miguel was already dead before they fled together, which was not the case. *Coño* was betrayed a few months later by "El Barba", Leonard Schneider, a SIFA agent.[48] *Coño* was shot and arrested on December 5; he was savagely tortured and died two days later. He was 31 years old.

---

48 Schneider had, according to some, infiltrated MIR already during the Unidad Popular period. Others believe that Barba was turned and became a traitor when he was first arrested by the SIFA and tortured after the coup.

At home in my house *Marco Antonio* and I discussed the implications of Miguel´s death but it was hard to actually understand the consequences. Around a week later *Marco Antonio* left my house and my routines would soon be turned upside down. Before that happened I was able to send a letter to my friends in Sweden:

I write this letter to you after the black day of the 5th of October when our secretary general Miguel Enriquez was assassinated.

"Mejor morir de pie que vivir de rodillas" (Better to die upright than to live on your knees)

All of us, all the people feel sadness and anger. But he died a hero: after having been ambushed by 68 soldiers and intelligence agents, with heavy (50 caliber) artillery, …it is thanks to the strength of at least three of my compañeros and personal friends, that have been arrested and savagely tortured, (and not said a word to give me away) that I can continue doing what I am. The best way to honor their courage is to keep on . And I feel totally identified with our struggle. Today, here in Chile, I feel happier and more satisfied with my life than I have ever done before. Day by day, minute by minute, I feel strengthened in my belief, in my decision to stay and fight. I know that our struggle is necessary, because it is more than justified and because history demands it. …… he and three other compañeros fought and upheld them for nearly three hours. He died with his weapon in his hand. He didn't die in vain. Already there is someone who has picked up his weapon to continue the struggle. All of us, although we feel this terrible blow deeply, at the same time feel strengthened in our revolutionary conviction. He has showed us the way. He didn't flee out of the country with his tail between his legs, although he was probably the most wanted man in Chile. He stayed side by side with the workers, the farmers, the slum-dwellers and the students, to share their lot of misery and oppression and above all to share in the struggle against the gorillas49 for a revolutionary society. To be a militant of the MIR entails a complete devotion to the struggle even to the point of death. The struggle requires this. The struggle re-quires an avant-garde,….Our responsibility as a party is great but it can and is providing leadership. In Chile today, through the Resistance Committees, MIR is the only party which is functioning well, and although we have suffered important losses, we already have a massive and a steadily increasing support from the masses. The oppression is severe. Many compañeros have been tortured and killed. The junta has declared an open war against MIR specifically "because it is the most dangerous". But the compañeros are strong and the great majority of those who have been tortured have not said a word. It is possible to withstand torture if your conviction is strong enough".

"Miguel la Resistencia Popular triunfará. Hasta la Victoria siempre!
(Miguel, the Popular Resistance will triumph. Until Victory, always!)

---

49 *the term used by MIR for the dictatorship

"La Clandestinidad" – life underground

Towards the end of 1974 I needed to move once again. Anita had become aware that there was a military officer living close by, with guards outside his house both day and night, to my house on Calle Bustos. When we understood this, Dago and I agreed that it was time to move. Living close to such a neighbor was an unnecessary risk. In these circumstances, Dago gave me a new task. MIR's new General Secretary, Andres Pascal Allende, needed a safe house for his closest assistant Lautaro. The proposal was that I should rent a new house and move in with Lautaro, so that we would appear to be a couple. My role as "palo blanco" at that time was the most valuable role that I could have for MIR, since there was a constant shortage of safe houses. I didn't question that.

Together with Andrés wife, Mary Ann Beausire, nicknamed within MIR as "la Chica" – I don 't recall her political name – we revised the ads for houses for rent. Mary Ann had European heritage and she was blond which proved significant later on. We identified the best house from a security standpoint. It was a small townhouse in an upper middle-class neighborhood close to the Avenida Tobalaba which we deemed was useful for our purpose. I presented myself to the owner as an international public servant employed at ECLA, and there was no problem in renting the house. No questions were asked. The Chilean upper class was – and still is – quite racist. In their eyes a blond European who seemed to have a lot of money was a bargain. The move was going to take place soon, at the start of November. I met *Lautaro* shortly before the planned move. It would be a very long time before I met Dago again.

That fateful day, Saturday November 2, started for me by a trip to the closest food store, which was an "ALMAC" on the corner of Avenida Bilbao and Jorge Matte Street. I was going to shop for food for the coming week and so far, everything was perfectly normal. Inside the store, which was quite large, I discovered "la Chica". She was there for the same purpose. We recognized each other but didn´t greet. All of a sudden, we heard gunshots outside, on the street. We both rushed out and stayed close to one another.

Lautaro, whose real name was Claudio Rodriguez Muñoz[50], had driven Mary Ann to the food store, parked outside and stayed in the car while she went inside to do the shopping. Without them being aware of it it, a DINA agent had recognized the car. It was a red Renault that had already been identified as the car of Andres Pascal Allende and DINA was searching for it. So, when the DINA agent, who wasn´t on duty, saw the car he nevertheless followed it. *Lautaro* parked and the unarmed DINA agent turned to a Carabinero who was guarding a house nearby. That house belonged to general Toro Davila, who was a minister in Pinochet´s government. The agent explained the situation to the Carabinero, who then followed him to the parking area and ordered *Lautaro* to get out of the car. *Lautaro* started to get out of the car but was able to get out his gun. He fired in self-defense and attempted to flee. The wounded policeman then shot at *Lautaro*, who fell down on the street and appeared lifeless. Two soldiers who were General Toro Davila's security guards, heard the shots and came running. *Lautaro*, badly wounded, managed to throw the hand grenade that he was carrying. One of the soldiers shot *Lautaro* in the head. *Lautaro* was taken to a hospital, but he was so badly wounded that he died shortly after. *Lautaro* was 22 years old.

When Mary Ann and I left the store and saw *Lautaro* on the street with blood running from his head we both immediately assumed

---

50 This information was shared by Andres Pascal Allende in a private message in June 2022

that he was already dead. We understood that we needed to get away as soon as possible. We went to my car and left rapidly. We also understood that we had probably been observed since the military and police had already gathered outside the store. We decided that we should try to get rid of the car and leave it. We managed to find a side-street some eight or ten blocks away where there was another FIAT, which was the same model and of a similar color and parked behind it. We separated and went different ways, after having first agreed to meet up the following day so I could get instructions on what to do. I went to my new house where I had already taken my few belongings, some knick-knacks from Peru and my clothes as bedclothes. That night I didn´t sleep much. I was shocked and nervous. The next day everything would change for me.

When I got up the next morning and looked out my window, I saw a car at the end of the street that looked like the kind of cars used by DINA. I also saw some men get out of the car and apparently force their way into the house on the corner. That was very ominous, and it terrified me. My first thought was that DINA was now searching for me and were going to search house by house. Maybe an informer had spotted my car previously when I had moved in and had alerted DINA. The car had an unusual turquoise color and stood out, so it wasn´t unreasonable to suppose that a neighbor had noticed it. That would mean that the car had been found where Mary Ann and I had left it, and that it had been identified. I needed to get out fast. Later I would learn that the car had, in fact, been found the day of the ALMAC shoot-out, and that DINA had gone to the address where the car was registered, namely Tom´s house. That house had been searched and of course my name was then put on the "wanted" list. It was clear that DINA wanted to get ahold of me.

Back at the house I decided to leave as quickly as possible. I remember that the fear I felt made my legs shake and I felt as though

I was hardly able to stay upright. I tied the kind of scarf that Chilean housewives used on my head, and I put on large sunglasses. In a large handbag I put one or two changes of clothes and sneaked out the back door. After having walked a few blocks with a pounding heart – I forced myself to walk slowly although I really wanted to run – I made my way to the meeting point where I was to meet Mary Ann. When we met, we had a short but very serious conversation. She suggested that I should go to the Swedish Embassy. However, I had already made up my mind and I told her that I wanted to stay and continue working for the resistance. For me, it was out of the question to seek refuge in the Swedish Embassy and I didn´t want to be treated differently from the other *compañeros* in MIR. I understood that I would need to go underground but I felt prepared to do that. Mary Ann promised to relay my reply to Andrés, and we decided on a new meeting later that day; it wouldn´t be with Mary Ann so I needed to carry a "santo y seña" for contact with the next person. Mary Ann was a very wanted person herself and needed to be on the streets as little as possible.

I don´t really remember very much of what I did the rest of that day except that I paid a visit to Guillermo, one of Tom´s friends at ECLA whom I had met during my first month in Santiago. At Guillermo´s place I was served lunch and we were able to talk for a number of hours. He was very unhappy with my decision to stay in the country, but he respected it. He was a nice man in his forties with left sympathies who was still a bachelor and lived with his elderly parents. During the afternoon at Guillermo´s house I wrote a resignation letter to ECLA stating that my father had suddenly taken ill and that I needed to be with him in Europe. Guillermo promised to take the letter to ECLA.

Later that day I met my contact who turned out to be *Alba*, whose real name was Diana Aron Svigilsky. She was a young Jewish journalist and a MIR member with important responsibilities on the national level related to intelligence. She told me that my request to go underground had been accepted and she took me to an apartment where I was to stay until my new identity papers had been arranged. For me Diana felt like an older sister taking care of me. She was warm and caring, and I rember that she had a lovely smile. Even though the whole situation was very frightening, she gave me confidence.

Diana Frida Aron Svigilisky
detenida por DINA
18 de Noviembre 1974

Now it was my turn to use a safe house. It was an apartment with almost no furniture. Two women lived there and worked during the daytime so I didn't see much of them. I stayed about a week. There was nothing to sleep on, so I put out some newspapers directly on the floor. Luckily it was spring so the weather wasn't cold. Diana helped me to change my appearance. She cut and dyed my hair dark brown, and she also got me some new clothes, a skirt, and a blouse of good quality in a style I wouldn´t have chosen myself but was meant to blend in with Santiago's middle class population. Getting me new identity papers was an important issue, but Diana told me that the workshop where they had been produced had been destroyed so production was down for the time being. Much later I understood that the comrade who was responsible for those logistics had fallen earlier in September. Carabineros often stopped people and checked their ID, so it was necessary to have one under a different name of course, if one was underground and had to be out on the streets. During the whole time that I was to remain in Chile I never got my fake ID.

After a week I went to stay in another place. This time it was a humble little house, more of a shack really, in one of the bigger shantytowns. It could have been Nueva La Habana but I wasn´t told. Diana took me there and again it was only meant to be a very temporary refuge. Those who received me were a young couple with a little son. Because the space was very small, I shared the boy´s bed, which he didn´t find odd at all. It was obvious that they were quite poor, and the main food consisted of bean soup. They were extremely good and generous people, and very courageous. I will be forever grateful to them. They were in fact risking their lives for me, an unknown comrade, but they were MIR sympathizers and part of the resistance movement. Had my presence been discovered they risked being arrested and maybe tortured. I stayed inside in the small bedroom and didn´t go out; even with that obvious safety measure, the danger was that the little boy would talk about me to his friends and that word would spread about my presence. I was a foreigner in that environment and it was urgent to find a different place to stay.

I never met Diana again. Diana was already a very wanted person when I met her the first time. She fell into the DINA´s hands on November 18, and was wounded as she tried to flee. She was taken to Villa Grimaldi, but she had a gunshot wound in one lung and another in a kidney, so she was then taken to one of DINA´s clinics in the Santa Lucia neighborhood. After that she disappeared. According to witnesses she was savagely tortured before she died. Testimonies in the trials against Krassnoff Martchenko, that would take place many years later, identified him as the person responsible for the torture of Diana. Krassnoff had led the fatal attack against Miguel Enriquez. Krassnoff was one of the worst of DINA´s assassins and would many years later be condemned to a lengthy prison sentence. Diana´s father was a well-known businessman and was in Israel when Diana was taken by the DINA, and as soon as he received this news, he called Pinochet directly to get her freed but by then it was already too late. Diana´s boyfriend, Luis Muñoz Gonzales, was arrested in December and taken to Villa Grimaldi where he was tortured; he was told that Diana was still alive and if he wanted to save her life, he needed to give DINA the information they wanted. Diana was 24 when she was killed.

After about a week in the shantytown, I was picked up by another comrade, whom I think was *Coño Alberto*. He was later arrested but was released and deported to Spain as he had double Chilean-Spanish citizenship.

My new safe house was a townhouse where a divorced woman lived together with her grown-up daughter and a housekeeper. I was told to keep my eyes closed as we drove to the house, since I wasn´t supposed to know where I was going. This happened each time I changed house; it was important that I not know where I had been so if I was to fall, the people who had sheltered me would not be identified. My contact from then on, and for some time, would be *Nancho* (Hernan Aguiló). Without asking questions I understood that the family I was staying with had known *Nancho* well for long time and trusted him. My cover story for the housekeeper, was that I was a distant relative to the family and that I needed rest since I had been ill.

It was summer by now and warm outside, but I stayed inside to avoid being seen by curious neighbors. Even in this family, the housekeeper probably understood more than we told her, but she was loyal and kept her silence. Nancho came to visit me now and then and promised to soon give me tasks that I could carry out. I received a letter from Dago who asked me to be patient. He tried to give me encouragement and told me to trust *Nancho*. By now it was December and Santiago was hot and humid.

During this time, we received terrible news. It was communicated with massive headlines by the media whoreported that the intelligence services had identified some "extremists" and that they had been shot to death openly on the street. This happened of December 3, 1975. The two "extremists" were Nano and Ana María. Nano and Ana María had been driving their car to the kindergarten to pick up their son, Alvaro. A block away from the kindergarten they were recognized by police in a patrol car. The police opened fire and shot them both to death. A relative of the couple heard the news on the radio and immediately went to the kindergarten to pick up the little boy. In the company of relatives Alvaro was taken abroad and grew up with his uncle, Nano´s brother, in Venezuela. Nano was 24 years old at the time of his assassination and Ana María 25. This news was a terrible shock and it affected me deeply as I felt that I had become close to these two compañeros.

Alejandro de la Barra and Ana María Puga

Within MIR a discussion had taken place after the coup, about what they should do with the member´s children. There was no joint decision, but some compañeros chose to send their children abroad with relatives once they themselves went underground. Others chose to keep the children with them, but many had traumatic experiences. It was a hard choice and there was no right or wrong.

When it was time for New Year's Eve, I managed to get help to send a short telegram to my parents in Spain. I wished them Happy New Year and signed it with my childhood nickname Mulle so that they would know that it came from me. Soon afterwards the house owner, her daughter and the housekeeper went on a holiday to the coast, and I stayed on in the house alone. This was a problem because I had to keep very quiet and not turn on any lights at night that could be seen from the outside.

On January 6 1975, in the "Diario Official", which was the official government paper that published decisions and announcements, I was pointed out with my name. It said that I was a member of MIR and that my political name was Marianne. Had DINA somehow confused me with Mary Ann? It said that my car had been seized and that the car had been used at a hold-up in a food store where I had been spotted with a known MIR leader. Anyone with information of my whereabouts was urged to contact the police….It was a mixture of mostly lies and some truth. In any case I had no knowledge of this at the time, but was told about it much later by Tor Sellström.

Now *Nancho* would come by every other or every third day. He told me that the situation was very serious and that many compañeros had fallen. He said that the party was in a process of re-organization and taking steps to increase security measures. Gradually I came to understand that even *Nancho* had lost contact with MIR´s leadership, but it didn´t seem to worry him so much. His approach was that it was necessary to lie low for a while. By now I was a bit restless because of the inactivity. I felt like I was hanging in the air, and I missed Dago. It was a very peculiar situation, but I got courage from Nancho who was being very stoic. He used to entertain me by telling me about MIR´s history and anecdotes, especially during the time before the Unidad Popular. We mostly talked about politics, both regarding Chile and international events. I read books that I found in the house and time passed.

One day *Nancho* came by and told me that he had found a safer place for me. He appeared to be concerned about the security in the townhouse. This time I was taken to a modest apartment on ground level with a small patio that wasn´t visible from the street. At last, I could sit outside and breathe fresh air. An elderly couple lived in the apartment, together with the man´s brother. The three of them were also supporters of the resistance movement. They liked to talk but even though they were very curious about me, they resisted the temptation to ask me questions about myself. They understood why I needed their help and protection and that was enough for them. I remember very well how we used to sit outside in the patio in the afternoon and evenings, drinking "yerba mate" and listening to tangos on the radio. The time I spent with them helped me to calm me down, but I was still worried about the fact that I didn´t have my ID papers and that I wasn´t doing anything useful. One day Nancho stopped coming. After waiting for some days, I decided that the time had come for me to leave. I took farewell of the elderly trio and left their place with a few belongings in a cloth bag.

Now the problem was that I really didn´t have anywhere to go and that DINA were searching for me. I decided to turn to my friend Stephanie in order to try to work out something from her place. Stephanie was very surprised when I turned up at her place but soon understood in general terms what had happened and received me with open arms. I stayed a week or two with her and after that I was able to find a new place to stay, but before that something happened that shocked us both.

On February 19 – this was now 1975 – Chilean television transmitted, an unusual press conference which had been pre-announced only a day or two before. It was supposed to be something sensational and a victory for the regime. To my dismay I saw four men sitting at a table with a big sign saying, "Leaders of MIR" and among them was *Marco Antonio*, or José Hernan Carrasco, who had been staying at my house only a few months earlier. There were three others beside him: Humberto Menanteau, Hector Hernan González and Cristian Mallol. The message from the four was a call to everyone in MIR to give up. They stated that the resistance battle was lost, that MIR had been crushed and that surviving MIR members should lay down their arms and abandon the struggle. Their message was shameful. No-one in MIR took this message seriously; it was obvious that it had been coerced and that the four had been subjected to torture that they hadn´t managed to stand up to it. MIR´s response was harsh; the four were named as traitors. This was what appeared in the March number of El Rebelde, which had a relatively extensive underground distribution[51] :

"In the face of torture or death, MIR keeps silent and doesn´t betray, and anyone who talks is a traitor to the party and to the working class. The party condemns traitors to death and will see to it that the sentence is carried out. Almost all our fallen compañeros have shown an exemplary attitude in the face of torture and death. Many heroes from our party and from the working class have shown, by giving their lives, that it is possible to face torture until death when you are a true revolutionary. But since September 11 and until now almost one hundred who have sought asylum have been expelled from our party; a very small group have deserted and betrayed. They will be executed. We announce the names of this group of abominable people who have bought their lives through dirty betrayal. They are sentenced to death and any Chilean or revolutionary anywhere in the world has the right to carry out this sentence."[52]

Later we would know that both Carrasco and Menanteau had been arrested at the end of December the year before, and that, after having been subjected to torture by DINA, they had agreed to take part in the press conference. After that they were kept in Villa Grimaldi but separated from the other prisoners. They were released in September 1975 and attempted to contact MIR´s leadership in an unsuccessful intent to explain and make amends. DINA found out about this and both Carrasco and Menanteau were re-arrested on November 20, and again taken to Villa Grimaldi. Both

---

51 I saw this text with my own eyes much later
52 "El Rebelde" No. 104, March 1975

were executed by DINA on December 1. So, in the end it was DINA and not MIR that executed them. Carrasco was 28 years old and Menanteau was 24. Mallol was held prisoner in different concentration camps like Tres Alamos and Puchuncaví for a long time and finally released. He was isolated by the imprisoned Miristas in the camps and wound up reaching out to another party on the Left, who took him in. González left Chile after having been held prisoner for a long time and went to Europe. The death sentence against them was never carried out, but they were considered as traitors by MIR members. Many years later the opinion regarding the four has been mitigated and they are regarded primarily as victims.[53]

This maneuver by the dictatorship was part of the strategy of psychological warfare ,it directed against MIR. The purpose of the televised press conference on February 19, 1975, was primarily to demoralize those that continued to fight back. Similar tactics were used in Brazil and later in Argentina. Apparently, DINA thought that some would actually give up as a result of this message, but that didn´t happen.

Much, much later I would find out that during the week or weeks when I had gone underground in November of the year before, the Swedish Embassy had received a telephone call. Carl Johan Groth, who was Chargé d´affaires at the Embassy[54], took the call. The person calling said that he was from MIR and that he wanted to inform them that I had been arrested. He requested the Embassy to act quickly to have me released. At that point Groth wasn´t aware of what had happened to me and immediately turned to the Chilean Ministry of Foreign Affairs demanding my release. The Ministry denied any knowledge of my whereabouts and relatively

53 From "Olvidos y recuerdos de un montaje comunicacional" by María Olga Ruiz
54 After the expulsion of Edelstam Sweden didn´t have an ambassador in Chile. The Embassy was managed by a Chargé d´affaires.

soon it became clear that I was not under arrest. So, the question was, why had DINA made the fake call? The simple answer was that DINA was trying to find out where I had gone; if the Embassy didn´t act it would mean either that I was within the premises of the Embassy or that I had left the country with a fake passport and that the Embassy had helped to get me out. Groth's action meant that he didn´t know where I was either and that meant I was probably still in Chile. DINA continued to search for me now that my link to MIR was established.

On the 21st of February I wrote a letter to my friends in Lund so that they could pass it on to the Chile committee in Stockholm. Stephanie helped me send it. This time I wrote in Swedish, by hand:

Friends -

I have received news that at the beginning of January someone in Berlin called the Chile committee in Stockholm and said that I had been taken prisoner and that someone was supposed to have seen me in the concentration camp Tres Alamos. I found out about this only a few days ago and am sorry that this fake message has been sent to you. I remain in freedom and have up to now not seen the inside of the gorilla torture chambers.

The reason for this misunderstanding is that I had to go underground in November of last year, and I haven´t had the possibility to contact the Swedish Embassy or my friends and inform them that I am fine and without any major problems. I am aware that I am being searched for, but this applies to most of the people in the resistance movement. So, I sincerely hope that no-one had taken any action on my behalf.

My intention is to stay and continue working for the resistance movement. The political conditions for the continued struggle against the dictatorship are positive which I´m sure you are aware of. The catastrophic economic situation, the miserable salaries for the working class, the vast unemployment, the gorilla dictatorship which only has support from the wealthy upper class, the class hatred on the part of the proletariat. In contrast the situation for the resistance movement itself is very troublesome. We have lost many leaders. They have been tortured to death and assassinated; many have fallen but there have also been some deserters who have preferred asylum to participation in the struggle. However, the struggle itself creates new leaders and with each passing day more join the resistance at grassroot level. Our perspective is long term. Only when the resistance is a mass movement will we be able to overthrow the dictatorship.

The international solidarity is incredibly important. Material and moral support is enormously significant and is much appreciated by everyone here. Not even newspapers like El Mercurio55deny that Chile has a bad reputation internationally and that the strong solidarity movement is a fact in Europe, USA, and Latin America.

I want to stress that this is a personal letter. I turn to you so that you can inform the Chile Committee that it needs to abstain from any action on my behalf, if any such are being planned. I think about you, hope that you are well and that you continue with your valuable work. Many hugs and greetings …

---

55 The major right-wing newspaper

At the same time, I wrote a letter directly to the Swedish Embassy with more or less the same message.

Unknown to me Tor had written the following letter dated February 2, which was some weeks before my own letter, to Carl Johan Groth at the Swedish Embassy:

Dear Carl Groth:

After a conversation with Ingmar Karlsson at the Swedish Ministry for Foreign Affairs, I am sending you this letter regarding Ann Stödberg.

Ann Stödberg if a close friend of mine…immediately after the military coup in September 1973, I met with Ann in Paris and we have been in contact since then, first in Peru and now in Chile. Our contact was broken – or better said: we have been unable to write to one another since June 1974. After that date I have received sporadic reports of Ann´s situation through joint friends in Lund and other parts of Sweden.

At the end of November, I received the information that Ann had supposedly been arrested or had disappeared. As the international secretary to the Swedish Chile Committee, I have tried to have this information verified through the Chilean left, without letting it become public. At the same time, I have reached out to the Swedish Ministry of Foreign Affairs. I have thus been able to follow developments relatively well and consider – from this far-off horizon- that your approach of not making Ann´s case a public matter, to be correct. However in the last weeks more information on Ann´s situation (in general) has reached Europe. This fact, together with the fear that Ann could become a new Raul Wallenberg[56], changes the situation. It is for this reason that I am writing you this letter, and with the hope that you can let us know as soon as possible, what your opinion is regarding this matter.

As you are aware the military Junta issued a Decree on December 13 according to which Ann is supposed to be a member of MIR. She was supposed to have been involved in a robbery of a food store and her car has been seized. The Decree was published in the "Diario Oficial" on January 6, 1975. Through this Decree the case is public. More or less at the same time Ann´s disappearance/arrest has been confirmed by refugees arriving from Chile. Her disappearance/arrest was commented on during the Second Russel Tribunal in Brussels, and according to information received, her name is now on the Chilean Left´s list of disappeared persons, a list which has been given to Amnesty International.

Against the background that a) Ann in fact has disappeared b) her case has been made public by the Junta and c) the formal and informal contacts with both the Chilean government and the Chilean Left´s organizations in Chile and in Sweden have not rendered any positive results, I have, together with others who are aware of the case, come to the conclusion that a public campaign would not hurt and could instead save Ann´s fate from a death that many of us fear may already have occurred.

Within the framework of the campaign that currently is taking place in Europe for disappeared people in Chile, as well

---

56 In the sense that Wallenberg disappeared after having been captured by Russian soldiers in 1945. His remains have never been found and his fate remains unknown.

as for women prisoners, we have decided to start a campaign for Ann Stödberg. In our understanding it is now only international public opinion – in this case the Swedish public opinion – that can save her, as in previous cases others like Carmen Castillo and others have been saved.

With the hope of hearing from you as soon as possible I send you my warmest regards

Tor Sellström

I received a copy of this letter directly from Tor much later when I had returned to Sweden.

Still in Stephanie´s house and after having thought about my options, I reached out to a former colleague at ECLA. This was Eduardo V., a very nice family man with Left sympathies and whose house I had visited at the start of my time in Santiago. I called him and asked if I could come by and pay him a visit; he wasn´t aware of what had happened – only that I had suddenly quit my job – but of course he had a suspicion of what my visit might be about. He also understood that he was taking a risk by meeting with me, but he agreed to my visit. So I went to his place and briefly explained my predicament, and wondered if there was any way he could help me without putting himself or his family in danger. It didn´t take long for him to give me an answer. He consulted his cousin Nana and her husband Samson who lived on a small suburban farm – in Chile it´s called "parcela"-, at the very end of Avenida Departamental right on the southern outskirts of Santiago. Ironically it turned out that their farm was right across the street from the shanty town formerly known as Nueva La Habana (*Mickey´s* home, and where he had been a leader). Both Nana and Samson agreed to help me. Samson was an old communist, but he had a generous attitude with regard to the resistance movement.

Eduardo V drove me to their place, and I moved in. Once again, I had found a sanctuary. Nana and Samson were incredibly caring and thoughtful. Quite a lot of people lived on the farm, starting with Nana, Samson and their children from earlier marriages and their own son, as well as the farmworkers and others who worked there in various capacities. They were all told that I was a distant cousin from the south who had come to stay for some time. Samson had a vegetable stand at the "Vega Central", the central market in the center of the city, the, where he went every day to oversee the commerce. Although Samson was disabled due to polio in his childhood and had to go everywhere in a wheelchair or balancing on crutches, he had an enormous amount of physical energy. He also had quite a temperament! He could easily lose his temper. We often quarreled over politics, but it never affected his attitude towards me which was always kind and affectionate. I was given a room in a small bungalow at the back of the main house which was very useful as I could stay out of the way of visitors. It surprised me that he wasn´t subject to persecution since his political affiliation was well known, but I assumed that his physical disability gave him an aspect of inoffensiveness. This family has a big place in my heart; the generosity of Samson and Nana, the warmth and support that they gave me was way beyond what I could have expected or hoped for.

Some news that we could rejoice in together was the end of the Vietnam war. That was spectacular, and it gave us added courage. It showed that the struggle against a powerful aggressor could be won even if it took a long time. Other international events that marked historical changes that were very encouraging were the Carnation Revolution in Portugal April 1974 (A Revolução dos Cravos), that marked the end of many years of military rule; the liberation and independence of the Portuguese colonies in Angola, Mozambique and Guinea Bissau that followed the Carnation Revolution. Of these three African countries only Guinea Bissau gained its independence through a military victory over the Portuguese troops. Many years later I would live and work in Guinea Bissau together with Juancho and our four children.

In the farmhouse I didn´t only talk with Samson and Nana, but also to their daughters. The youngest daughter Francisca was a high school student and by and by she confided to me something that not even her family was aware of.She was herself active in the student resistance movement that was connected to MIR. The work she carried out was mostly spreading propaganda materials against the military junta. She had understood by what I said to Samson, without it being mentioned openly, that I belonged to MIR. She was extremely focused and mature for her age and finally I felt that I could try to send a message through her, to try to re-connect to Dago. It was risky but worth a try.

So I sent a message addressed to Quintullanca (which was by now his political name). She handed it over to a comrade who was her superior, and then the message travelled upwards in the chain until it reached Dago. After a week a received a return message; I was told to meet a compañero closer to the center of the city, carrying a "santo y seña" recognition signal. I did this and after a few attempts, I was approached by a compañero who was known as "the priest" ("El Cura") who had that nickname since he had at one time studied theology. His real name was German de Jesus Cortés Rodriguez, but I knew him as Ricardo. From Ricardo I received instructions that came from Dago, to leave the farm and temporarily go to stay in a house with a Dutch family. They worked at one of the UN institutes in Santiago and I stayed there with them for a few weeks. Dago had written that we were soon going to be able to move in together at last in a new house, which we did. When we finally were able to meet again, he explained that even if Samson and Nana´ house appeared innocuous, he feared that the house could be raided by the military at any time which was why it had been a hurry to get me out of there. Dago was not the sort of person who heaped praise on anyone for what they had done but he did express his satisfaction with the fact that I had been able to manage the problems that had arisen since I went underground.

A short reprieve

So at some point in May of 1975, Dago and I were able to move in together in a house where the owner was out of the country for a longer period. It was a joyful reunion! We had been apart for more than half a year. Later we would find out that the owner of the house was a well-known Chilean economist, and a Christian Democrat, who had moved abroad. He was of course unaware of who would be living in his house. Dago and I could not go outside so *Ricardo* was our contact with the outside world. *Ricardo* would come by a couple of times a week and brought us food supplies and other necessities apart from exchanging information and documents with Dago.

In a certain way It was a kind of curious honeymoon, which I was happy for. Even Dago could relax to some extent. To my satisfaction I could also contribute with something. Dago would write his documents by hand, and I would type them. Dago´s texts were part of the documents that were produced by MIR´s leadership; they often contained analysis of the current situation and political positions regarding events, as well as providing different types of orientation to the *compañeros* in the resistance movement. We lived in this way for a few months. However, much too soon, we were forced to leave.

We didn´t talk much about the future anymore. Dago wanted me to leave Chile. His opinion, which was correct of course, was that as a foreigner I didn´t have any natural network that I could fall back on. I was very vulnerable due to my reliance on the good will of a few people and on the party.We had already experienced that it couldn´t always give the necessary support. Dago's thinking was that my vulnerability was a solid reason for me to leave the struggle in Chile and to instead make myself useful to MIR in Sweden. I didn´t want to listen to him and we stopped talking about it because it was hard to take a decision as long as we weren´t in agreement. Sometimes we talked about our fallen *compañeros* and *compañeros* and what they had had to face. Sometimes we talked about what awaited us if we were to fall. In spite of everything I couldn´t find it in me to think about leaving. It would have felt like a betrayal of those who had risked so much to help me. Who had hidden me at the risk of their own lives. And a betrayal of those compañeros who had lost their lives. My ties to Dago were by now known to DINA, so I couldn´t expect any mild treatment. Dago was very clear that he would not let himself be taken alive.

In mid-July we were made aware of some articles in the main newspapers that were terribly disheartening, both with regard to their content but also by the way the news had spread. At that point in time the term "fake news" was unknown, but this was an example of a gigantic set-up of orchestrated lies. It started with a newspaper in Brazil, the "Novo O´Dia", that printed a headline together with a long article that stated that 59 MIR members had died in an armed confrontation in Salta, Argentina. Following that article, the newspaper "Lea" in Argentina – a "newspaper" that in the same way as "Novo O´Dia", had only appeared on that one day and then never again – printed an article stating that 60 MIR members had been killed In Argentina in internal vendettas . The reactionary Chilean newspapers El Mercurio, La Segunda, La Tercera and Ultimas Noticias, then picked up this "news", and published it. So in total there was a list of 119 people who were reported as dead.

Most of them were MIR members who had been disappeared by the military Junta, but there were also a few members from the Chilean Socialist and the Communist parties. The headlines were as follows: "Exterminated as rats"; "Bloody internal battles among exiled MIR members in Argentina". What was particularly upsetting was that they also printed photographs of bodies that had been burnt or shot. The photos also showed the ID cards lying beside the bodies of those that had been killed, with the names of *compañeros* who had been disappeared in Chile. Long afterwards it was discovered that the bodies were of Argentinians killed by the Argentinian secret services, and that the ID cards had been provided by their Chilean counterparts. This whole macabre set-up – which we would also only find out much later – had been given the name Operation Colombo and had been organized by Alvaro Puga Cappa. Puga Cappa was the head of "civic issues" in Pinochet´s military junta as well as the head of psychological warfare in DINA. He himself wrote under a pseudonym in the newspaper "La Segunda". One of the 119 people was *Juancho´s* brother, Jorge Espinosa Mendez; another was Dago´s brother, Carlos Freddy Perez Vargas; and yet another was Pato´s brother, Isidro Miguel Pizarro Meniconi. All three had been disappeared the year before.

Operation Colombo was a part of the psychological warfare against MIR but probably also had another purpose. This was, as part of the preparation for the planned visit to Chile by the UN Commission on Human Rights, to cast doubts about the existence of disappeared persons. The visit which was ultimately postponed by the Junta. It was also an example of the cooperation between DINA and the Argentinian secret services which would develop into the Operation Condor.[57] Through this clumsy maneuver the Junta would try to claim that the people who had been disappeared had died in internal battles outside of Chile and that there were no disappeared persons in Chile. The cases of the 119 had already become known around the world and, internationally, the Junta´s version had no credibility whatsoever.

---

57 Se more about the Operation Condor in the chapter "The Operation Condor and the decades that followed"

Then one day when *Ricardo* came on one of his regular visits, we got to talking about how the house that we had been living in had been rented. *Ricardo* told us that a European woman had acted as "Palo Blanco". Since I knew some of the Europeans in Santiago – they weren´t so many by now – I asked for more details. It turned out to be my friend Stephanie. That was bad news. I knew that Stephanie had a heart of gold and was very courageous. The problem was that she not only helped MIR but also the Socialist Party and possibly some other Left parties. Since she was known to many people there was a very high risk that she would be discovered. Should she fall andbe subjected to torture there was a serious risk that she would give up information, including the information about the house that she had rented for us – without knowing of course who the "house guests" would be. Since the support she offered, in my opinion, was based on humanitarian reasons I believed that her capacity to withstand torture was probably less than that of the politically very motivated Chilean *compañeros. Ricardo* didn´t know Stephanie as well as I did. After a brief discussion Dago, *Ricardo* and I agreed that staying at the house was a potential risk , so we immediately prepared to leave[58].

Dago explained that I couldn´t go with him. There was no room for me where he was going. I had to return to the Dutch couple ´s house and from there assist in finding a new place to stay for both of us. Now that I was underground it felt like an impossible task, but Dago assured me that he had contacts and would guide me. We parted ways and *Ricardo* provided me with an AK 47 that I didn´t want, but that he insisted that I take in case I needed to defend myself. I would have preferred a gun but there was a scarcity of those. I hid the AK 47 under my bed and practiced taking it apart and putting it

[58] Unknown to us Stephanie left Chile for good early July because by then her situarion was very compromised

114

back together. Dago himself, unknown to me, had gone back to a small farm called Santa Eugenia about 30 kilometers outside Santiago between the villages Padre Hurtado and Malloco. Other MIR leaders were living on the farm: Andrés Pascal and his wife Mary Ann Beausire; Nelson Gutierrez and his wife Maria Elena Bachman and their little daughter Paula as well as Martin Hernandez who had been a MIR member for many years. Nelson and Maria Elena had been the first ones to live there: the others had come later. That three of MIR´s highest leadership were staying in the same place was a sign of how badly resources were stretched in regard to security. When Dago was forced to return it was only meant to be for a short while until we could find another place to go, but then the catastrophe occurred.

For several months we attempted to find a new place to stay. I had no network of my own, so I depended on Dago´s instructions to reach out to various of his contacts. One after one my attempts failed. The prospects of finding a safe house appeared bleak.

Dago and I wrote to one another regularly, at least once and often several times a week. Our patient postman was *Ricardo*. I still have some of these messages:

Quintullanca (Dago) to Claudia:

…after long and detailed instructions on contacts to be taken for the house hunting task, he writes the following (see translation below):

Te pido lo que solo lo que a un militante de confianza muy grande podría pedirle y tú sabes porque. Solo la mirada fría y objetiva sobre la realidad nos permite ser eficaces para cambiarla. Si perdemos esa perspectiva ganamos lazos, que construidos sobre realidad falsa, nos duelen y nos frustran.

En concreto te pido porque te quiero mucho que no olvides nuestras conversaciones sobre nosotros y "la vida"….es todo por hoy. Te quiero y te admiro cada día más tu calidad militante. Y te pido no olvides que soy como tú dices, "un huaso malo". Cariños, besos y saludos revolucionarios. -

Quintullanca

Translation:

I ask of you only that which can be asked of a combatant of greatest confidence and you know why. Only a cold and objective view of reality will allow us to change it. If we lose that perspective, and build on a false reality, we create expectations that hurt and frustrate us. In concrete terms I ask you because I love you very much, to not forget our conversations about us and about "life". That´s all for today. I love you and for each day that passes I admire more your qualities as a combatant. And I ask you to not forget that I am, as you say, a "huaso malo" (a mean cowboy). Hugs, kisses and revolutionary greetings. -

Quintullanca

The attack in Malloco

Renato, the son of the owners of the farm and who acted as the link between the leadership on the farm and the rest of the MIR, had been arrested after a tip-off. Renato was above-ground, so his papers were legitimate and the address of the farm was on his identity card.The farm where Andrés, Mary Ann, Nelson, María Elena and Dago were staying had come to DINA´s attention.

There were several buildings on the farm: the owners, the Garrido family, lived in the biggest house as well as Martin Hernandez, a member of MIR's central committee. Martin´s main task was to compile and edit the documents on strategy that were produced by the Political Commission. Andres, Mary Ann, Nelson, María Elena, their little baby Paula, and Dago were at the time living in a smaller house where, normally, the administrator of the farm would stay. On the evening of October 15, the farm was surrounded and attacked with firearms by the DINA´s Caupolican Operative Brigade, commanded by the army captain Miguel Krassnoff Martchenko. A great number of heavily armed police (Carabineros)[59] from different police unts in the Metropolitan region of Santiago, as well as a helicopter and four armored vehicles MOWAG participated in the attack. [60] Initially it was the larger farmhouse that was the target of the attack which gave the MIR leadership a brief reprieve.

---

59 El Rebelde, special edition nr 111, October 1975
60 According to the judicial investigation many years later carried out by the Special Prosecutor for Human Rights violation Marianela Cifuentes, it was DINA´s Brigada Operative Caupolican led by Krassnof Martchenko together with a larger number of Carabineros from various different police precints in Santiago and the back-up of at least one helicopter, that carried out the attack in Malloco.

They had prepared themselves for a possible attack and there was a plan on how the defense could be managed. The first option was to actively defend themselves and then retreat with the help of a car. That meant that all of the adults had specific tasks in the defense plan. The retreat would take place with the car that was normally hidden in another smaller storage building, further away from the main entrance. Before the retreat the smaller administrator´s house was to be set on fire. In the house there were documents and arms. This part of the plan was executed successfully. The fire led to a massive explosion, which put a halt to the attacking forces and enabled an initial escape for the group. However, Dago had been seriously, perhaps already mortally, wounded when he and Nelson had tried to reach the car which, unusually, was parked close to the main farmhouse. He couldn´t continue with the others and by giving fire he covered their retreat.

Through the judicial investigation that took place many years later it was established that Dago died after having received a large number of ballistic projectiles fired from at least two weapons, a gun and a rifle, which wounded him in his head, his chest, his stomach, his right shoulder and his right leg.

Nelson had been shot in the leg but was able to get to the agreed meeting place. Andres, Nelson, Mary Ann, Maria Elena with baby Paula in her arms, were able to escape by first retreating among the cattle which shielded them, and then making their way away from the main buildings using the irrigation canals. Andres had badly twisted his ankle but with the help of the others he could keep up. In the darkness of the night, they hid in the riverbed of the river Maipo. At dawn they were able to leave the farm through an opening at the back and started walking on the nearby railroad tracks. There the escaping group met two women farmworkers who luckily proved to be Left sympathizers. The group warned them of the military forces ahead. The women agreed to take Paula, who they promised to care for very well. After that Andres, Nelson, Mary Ann and Maria Elena reached a small rural road where they stopped a car and forced the owner to turn it over to them, and then drove to Santiago. Martin Hernandez who had been in the big farmhouse had managed to escape as well. The Garrido family were arrested.[61]

Dago was killed that night.[62] His courageous action helped save the lives of the others.

The whole attack was transmitted, as it was unfolding, the same evening, on the Chilean television; the journalists had been fore-warned by the military about the attack, in order for them to be able to transmit it. I remember seeing the news where the names of the *compañeros* and *compañeras* were announced as escaping terrorists and falling into a state of shock. It felt like a nervous breakdown. Already early the next day *Ricardo* came and picked me up, for which I have been forever grateful.

After having remained hidden for a few days Andrés and Mary Ann entered the Costa Rican embassy where they requested asylum, while Nelson and Maria Elena ended up at the Papal Nunciature, the Vatican's embassy in Santiago. Two days after the events, the two women who had taken care of baby Paula handed her over to the Pro-Peace Committee (Comité Pro Paz)[63] , after which she was

---

61   The description of the events is based on my conversation with Andres
     Pascal Allende (August 2022) and Maria Elena Bachman (September 2022)
     In 2019 the justice system tried to make a reconstruction of the
     events in Malloco.
62. The trial finalized five years later in January 2024 with convictions.
63   The Comité Pro Paz was created in 1973 by the Christian churches together
     with the Mosaic congregations, and was active with the support of the
     Catholic Church. It was dissolved at the end of 1975 by Pinochet. The
     Church replaced it with the Solidarity Vicarage (Vicaría de la Solidaridad),
     which was active for the remainder of the 17-yearlong dictatorship

later re-united with her parents when they arrived at the Nuncia-ture. Nelson´s gunshot wound was taken care of by a British doctor, Sheila Cassidy. Dr Cassidy herself was arrested by DINA afterwards and taken to Villa Grimaldi where she was badly tortured. She was finally released and returned to the United Kingdom where she wrote a book about her experience.

Andrés and Mary Ann travelled to Costa Rica but later left for Cuba. Nelson, Maria Elena, and Paula left Chile in March 1976. They first travelled to Sweden and then later to Cuba some months later. Martin Hernandez hid in a nuns' convent but later in December he fell. He was released after some time, as was the Garrido family.

Dago´s body lay in the mortuary of the Institute of Forensic Medi-cine (Instituto Médico Legal) with the denomination NN (unknown) for two months even though his relatives tried to claim it for burial. In December 1975 the information was released that the "unknown body" had been buried in a mass grave at the General Cemetery. Dago´s mother Otilia received other information which wasthat Da-go´s remains had been buried in the plot 29 in the General Cem-etery, without specifying the exact place. Dago´s body was never recovered. His mother later denounced these circumstances to the UN Committee on Torture. Dago was 27 when he was killed.[64]

One year previously Dago had written a letter to his mother where he said:

> *"Otilia, nuestra justa decisión de permanecer en Chile es un acto consciente, estamos dispuestos a morir; no queremos morir, yo quiero vivir mucho, quiero ver el triunfo de la rev-*

---

64 Dago would have been 28 on the November 7, 1975

olución, pero estoy dispuesto a entregar mi vida si llega la hora."[65]

Translation:

Otilia, our decision to stay in Chile was correct and is a conscious decision; we are prepared to die; we don´t want to die, I really want to live, I want to see the triumph of the revolution, but I am prepared to give my life if that time comes.

In Dagos mother´s book[66] on her five children who were assassinated by the dictatorship, Andres Pascal Allende remembers Dago in the following way:

"Dago was a brilliant organizer and builder of the party, and as an internal leader of the political avantgarde. I don´t think there was any other leader within the party that had as much experience of internal organizational leadership as the one Dago exercised during the UP period….the complexity of Santiago´s Regional Committee wasn´t only due the dimensions or to the enormous amount of tasks that needed to be carried out. The Regional Committee was also politically complex, since its members were compañeros and compañeros with strong personalities, who had many opinions and positions, and even though they never led to fragmentation, the political discussions were intense…..Dago needed to mediate and lead the discussions in order to make sure that they led to concrete political action. He didn´t always agree with the Political Commission, he was considered as very stubborn ("cabeza dura") in his positions. Often it was necessary to give him many strong arguments to get him to change his

65 "La dictadura me arrebato´cinco hijos" by Otilia Vargas Perez
66 "La dictadura me arrebató cinco hijos" by Otilia Pérez Vargas

position....but he had total respect for collective decisions and for the Political Commission. So when decisions had been taken collectively by the leadership, he carried them out with great determination even if he didn´t agree with them. He was very well liked because he was very modest, both in his lifestyle and in his total dedication to party work. He was very demanding of his compañeros, but also open to having them express their opinions...Miguel (Enriquez) held him in high esteem and considered his opinions very seriously".

In a letter to me from *Gaspar* (Patricio Rivas) written in September 2022, where Gaspar remembers fallen *compañeros* and *compañeras*, among them Chico Perez, Diana, Germán and Dago, he writes the following with respect to Dago:

Dago: your understanding of the revolutionary task and the development of MIR, both in political as well as in ethical terms, was in some ways very classic. From the early episodes from the beginning of the twentieth century, episodes that were subversive and forceful. There were in these episodes' connections to the images that we had in our heads of the Bolsheviks in 1917 (that inspired us)....In 1971 when you were released from prison where you had been with other compañeros , you were nominated to be the Secretary of the party´s Regional Committee. It wasn´t easy to be the head of the Regional Committee, that consisted of many you, brilliant and dedicated Miristas who were profoundly engaged in the building of a new Left, in a Chile that was Left. To define society, politics and the revolution in a coherent way. You organized the Regional Committee and you gave it leadership and identity. In the collective tasks you showed your capacity for analysis and execution. We met often after the coup. In your words as well as in the directions you gave, you expressed – as did others-a great optimism. I was in my cell that day in October 1975 when our comrade Arturo Villavela told me about the confrontation that had taken place (between military forces and the MIR leadership) in Malloco, where there was a safe house. You stayed and covered the retreat of the other compañeros. You died in battle".

With the attack in Malloco MIR's leadership, at that point in time, had been destroyed. Andres and Nelson continued working from Cuba and the internal leadership in Chile was assumed by Hernan Aguilo (*Nancho*). *Nancho* was the *compañero* who had taken care of me during my first time underground, but now he had more important tasks. *Nancho* stayed underground, both in Chile and in other places in Latin America without ever being discovered, for almost twenty years. He abandoned his underground existence in 1994.

Report on the attack in Malloco: El Mercurio was – and still is – the biggest daily newspaper in Chile and is very right wing; the headlines.the photo and the content of the article are all grossly false; the article is yet another example of the attempts of the reactionary right wing forces to mislead and dupe the public. The photo supposedly shows Dago, although its a photo of another *compañero;* Dago was not the second in command in MIR; in the article it s stated that the security forces had found an underground prison in Mallocom that was supposed to have been built by the leaders of MIR for the purpose of torturing kidnapped people, etc. The story of Dago´s history in MIR is full of fabrications and falsehoods, for example that Dago had received military training in Cuba. Dago had never been outside the borders of Chile.

My last months in Chile

The day after the events in Malloco, *Ricardo* came to pick me up and take me to a safe house on Tobalaba where his *compañera Helena* lived. *Helena* was also underground. *Ricardo´s* action in coming to get me was gesture typical of *Ricardo´s* consideration and compassion.

The first weeks after Malloco were hard. I was very depressed. The "Palo Blanco" for the house was an old lady who came by daily. Both *Helena* and I were unable to go out and depended completely on her. There were neighbors close by so we had to be very careful not to make any sounds that could be heard by them. So, we moved around very quietly and spoke in low voices. *Ricardo* made sure that we were occupied; our task was to write and produce El Rebelde. We wrote the articles on a type-writer -this was long before computers – on a regular standard paper, and then we photographed the sheets a number of times and developed the films. The films were then packed in small packages and hidden in everyday products, "barretines", that *Ricardo* would take to compañeros for further distribution. The films were reproduced and spread in the resistance movement.

In one of the numbers of El Rebelde from that period there is a poem that I wrote. It is too long to reproduce here but it starts like this:

> *Te canto a ti*
> *Compañero desconocido*
> *camarada sin cara y sin nombre*
> *que has caído preso esta noche*
> *tan súbitamente*

como una piedra tirada al mar
tragada por las aguas obscuras
sin dejar otro rastro
que tu ausencia –
grito en el silencio
de la noche

Translation
I sing for you
my unknown comrade, my
faceless and nameless comrade
you who have fallen tonight and
disappeared
as suddenly as a rock thrown into the ocean
swallowed by the dark water
leaving no trace
except your absence –
silent scream
in the night

At some point we heard helicopters close by above the house on Tobalaba. That sound was usually a sign that DINA could be on its way to carry out an attack. *Helena* and I immediately started to make Molotov-cocktails that we placed in the living room. We also loaded our AK-47s. Thankfully the sound of helicopters faded away after a while and we could de-escalate the preparations. Still today I can feel my heartbeat increasing when I hear the sound of helicopters.

Then, at the end of December *Ricardo* informed me that a decision had been taken in the party leadership, which was headed by *Nancho*, and of which *Ricardo* himself was now a member, that I should leave Chile and continue working for the party abroad.

Helena should also leave Chile. Later I found out that this was due to her being pregnant. The other reason for this decision was that it was too costly to have a safe house only for the production of El Rebelde, which could be taken care of by others who weren´t as persecuted as *Helena* and myself.[67]

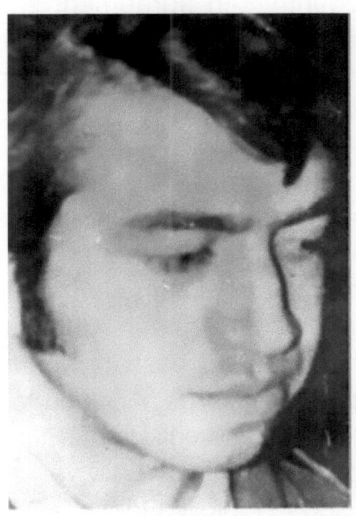

Germán de Jesus Cortes Rodriguez (Ricardo), "el Cura"

Ricardo and *Nancho* continued the struggle in Chile. *Nancho* survived but *Ricardo* (German Cortés) was taken prisoner by DINA in January 1978. He was viciously tortured and then shot in the back two days later. German was 29 years old when he was killed.

In the last week of December 1975, MIR reached out to the Swedish Embassy. A decision was taken on where I would be dropped at a certain hour on an agreed-upon day. So it happened and I

---

67 We knew that Helena´s relationship with *Ricardo* was known to DINA, as was my connection to *Nancho.*

was picked up by an Embassy employee who drove me to one of the Cuban houses that were still under Swedish protection. I was informed that I wouldn't be able to leave the country immediately because I would need a special permission, a "salvo conducto" (safe conduct). However, the Swedish Embassy would not be able to get me this permission since it needed to be requested by a Latin American country. An agreement existed with the Latin American countries to provide safe conduct permissions for each other's citizens if such were requested. The agreement didn't exist with other countries.

This meant that I needed to get into a Latin American embassy which was easier said than done. All the embassies were guarded by Carabineros in order to prevent presumed asylum-seekers from being able get access to the diplomatic premises. It was decided that I was to be smuggled into a Latin American embassy on New Year's Eve. The Venezuelan ambassador who was the doyen (eldest in service) in the Diplomatic Corps of Santiago, was hosting a New Year's party for his diplomatic colleagues. I was dressed up in a long dress and given make-up; my hair was put up in a makeshift hairdo. I was supposed to look like the wife of a Swedish diplomat and accompany him to the party. When we arrived at the ambassador's residence there were many Carabineros guarding it. But we were inside a CD-marked car and were not stopped. Once inside the house the Swedes informed the Venezuelan ambassador of my identity, and I was immediately sent up to the attic. In the attic there were some twenty other political refugees. When the Venezuelan embassy later requested the "*salvo conducto*" for me, they stated that I had entered the premises by jumping over the garden wall on another date. The Swedish Chargé d'affaires, Carl Johan Groth, visited me several times in the attic. First, he brought me clothes, later old Swedish newspapers to read and chocolate. At one point he told me that the Carabineros that had been in service on the night when

I had supposedly jumped over the wall, had been court-martialed for their negligence.

Unknown to me Tor Sellström´s and my paths were to cross again in an unexpected way at this time, which I would find out about later. In January 1976 it had been agreed by the Swedish Chile Committee that someone should travel to Chile to get a first-hand up-dated impression of the general situation and even to find out if the funds that had been collected by the Swedish Chile Committee had reached the intended beneficiaries. The person who would travel was Tor. Tor managed to borrow someone else´s passport and decided to cross the border between Argentina and Chile by bus at the Cristo Redentor crossing in the Andes. When he was about to fill in the immigration papers at the border control on the Chilean side, he looked up and saw a big poster with the word "Wanted" and a photo of me. Tor was shaken but was able to maintain his composure and managed to cross the border without problems. He didn´t know that at that point I was already safe at the Venezuelan residence.

We who sat in the attic remained there about six weeks before our salvo conductos were granted collectively, and we could leave Chile for our different destinations.

When the day came for me to leave in February 1976, I was picked up by Carl Johan Groth in his diplomatic car and driven to the airport, escorted by police on motorcycles. Groth followed me onto the airplane. I have no recollection of the trip back to Sweden. At Arlanda my two cousins, who had been informed of my arrival by the Swedish Ministry of Foreign Affairs were waiting for me, but they didn´t recognize me.

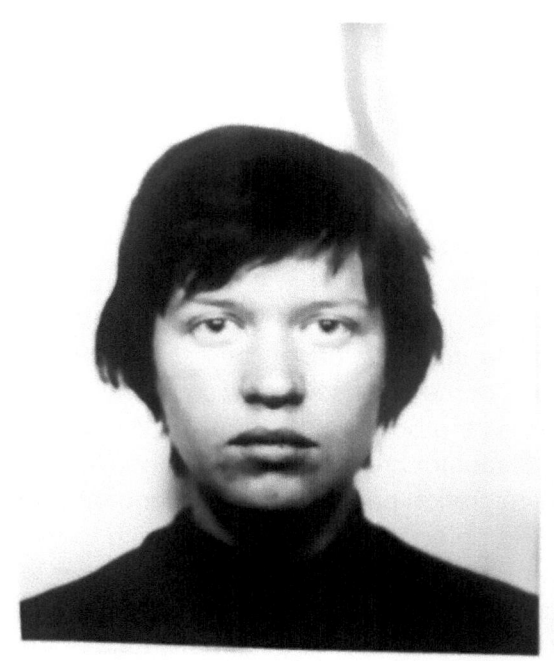

Back in Sweden

I met my cousins and myaunt and uncle during my first days back in Stockholm. Everything felt unreal. It was difficult for me to get used to being in a country where one could move around freely and where it wasn´t necessary to be constantly vigilant of one´s surroundings. It wasn´t so strange that my cousins hadn´t recognized me at Arlanda airport. I had lost around 15 kilos, my hair was cut short, dyed dark brown and my appearance , in general, was quite miserable. However, my appearance was nothing compared to how I felt. I travelled to see my parents who lived in Spain shortly after, since they had been frantic with worry on my account for a long time.

Pretty soon back in Sweden, I got a message that I was wanted in Paris. The person who wanted to see me was el *Gato*- the Cat – (René Venezuela), who was the MIR *compañero* responsible for the party´s logistics, so I went to Paris to report on all that I had been through. What Gato wanted to know above all were the details of my very last months in Santiago. His concern was to get an idea of the extent of the vulnerability that MIR was subject to at this point. Firstly, the assassination of Miguel had been a tremendous blow; the attack on Malloco and its consequences were another critical blow. Together with the death, disappearances, and imprisonment of numerous *compañeros* and *compañeras,* it was clear that MIR had suffered enormous losses.

Gato requested me to remain at the disposal of MIR in Sweden and help out with such tasks as were deemed necessary. I went back to Stockholm and wondered what I could do. Soon I received an instruction to rent a big apartment that would soon be needed to receive *compañeros* arriving from Chile. This felt familiar…although for this assignment I didn´t have to invent stories. As a Swede I could just rent an apartment openly, which at that time was easily done, so I rented a three-bedroom apartment in the southern suburbs, and soon after I received Nelson Gutierrez, his wife Maria Elena and baby Paula who had escaped from Malloco. Soon after that I also received Dago´s mother Otilia and Dago´s only surviving sister Patricia, who was 13 at the time. I remember Patricia as a very quiet girl.

Maria Elena, Nelson with little Paula and our compañero
"Tranquilo", Dr Alejandro Romero

Sometime later , we received *Juancho*. He had arrived in Stockholm directly from prison, where he had been held for a year after his trial. Juancho was very gaunt, marked by torture. He frequently suffered from nightmares. Our apartment was crowded by now, but Nelson considered that it was important that he stay with us, to feel part of the MIR community.

Juancho and I talked a lot and soon felt a connection in our sorrow. For me it was Dago´s death and for him it was the disappearance of his younger brother Jorge. To share sorrow gives comfort and creates special bonds. After some time our friendship developed into a relationship, but the intensity of the activities taking place obliged us to focus on other matters than ourselves.

Our apartment became the meeting point for those in MIR's leadership that were in Europe. They came and stayed; meetings were held. My role was to ensure the logistics; to make sure that there was food, drive people to different places in the second-hand car we had bought, act as a translator and interpreter, and at times help out with little Paula. I also took long walks with Otilia and Patricia and tried to give them some sense of normality. Nelson was very active; he held meetings not only with *compañeros* and *compañeras* from the party, but also with other members of the Chilean Left that were in Sweden. All those who were staying at the apartment were later going to leave for Cuba.

At the same time as there was intense activity in the apartment, I needed a real job and an income. Through the contacts that my *compañeros* had I was offered a job at the Cuban embassy in Stockholm as a translator and interpreter. To my great joy I found that my friends Tor Sellström and Lilian Inseth were already working there in the same capacity. Three full-time translators and interpreters proved to be cost that the embassy couldn´t carry and by fall all three of us had politely been asked to leave.

Maria Elena was pregnant with her second child and the due date for the baby´s birth was expected at the end of June. When the day arrived, I accompanied Maria Elena and was present until the baby was born. Maria Elena was a midwife herself, and everything went very smoothly. The baby boy was named Dagoberto.

Nelson participated in public gatherings as well, including a big meeting in Stockholm, where he spoke about the need, given the current circumstances in Chile, for the Left abroad to create what he called "una retaguardia estratégica" (a strategic rearguard). He meant that the most important task at this point in time was to gather forces and prepare for a long period of repression and authoritarian rule. Nelson was a perceptive analyst and understood the need for a long-term perspective on the struggle, in particular given the background of the heavy blows that MIR had suffered. Other members of the leadership were more anxious to return to Chile as soon as possible and participate actively in the struggle on the ground. Two years later in 1978, MIR's Central Committee took the decision to initiate the "Política de Retorno" (the Policy of Return).

In July 1976, a month after baby Dagoberto had been born, Nelson, Maria Elena, Paula, the baby, Otilia, Patricia, and Juancho all left for Cuba. The idea was that they were all, including Juancho, to stay there and not return to Sweden.

A few weeks after they had left, I received an unexpected phone call from Havana. It was the middle of the night for me and I wasn´t completely awake when I answered. It was *Juancho* calling and because I was still half-asleep I couldn´t stop myself from telling him that I was pregnant. He was very happy to hear this news and told me that he would immediately start preparations to return to Stockholm. This went against the expectations both of the Chilean *compañeros* and the Cubans. It wasn´t easy for him to come back but at last he was successful. It was a very big thing for both of us to be expecting a child; to create life almost seemed like an act of defiance against the background of all the deaths that we had witnessed. With time we had four children in all: Daniel, Rossana, Emilio, and Isabel.

Juancho and I in the fall of 1976

Juancho stayed on as an active member of MIR for some years but resigned from the Central Committee in 1978. His reasons for doing so were that he was against the "Policy of Return", and MIR´s plans to send compañeros back to Chile underground. Juancho was not against the return in itself, but he thought that it was way too early and he didn´t agree with the proposed methods for the struggle in Chile upon their return. He felt that it was a collective suicide. Instead, he took up his incomplete studies in physics and in 1984 he took his Master of Civil Engineering in Physics exam at the Swedish Royal Institute of Technology. For my own part, my engagement in political activities was naturally reduced with four small children to take care of at the same time as having a demanding job.

In Stockholm *Pato* (Francisco Pizarro Meniconi) was a close friend. He had been in prison with Juancho. *Pato* was one of the kindest people I have ever known and he was extremely helpful when the children were small. After some time, he chose to resume his activities in MIR even though he suffered from a debilitating illness. I met him in Santiago a few years back and we spent a day together; he died of his illness in September 2020.

Juancho and I also socialized with Tor and Lilian who had married and who remained good friends, although our paths would later go different ways due to our job postings in different parts of Africa. Tor and Lilian´s son Erik was the same age as our oldest son Daniel and when they were small, they played together. Lilian and I stayed in contact, and I visited her both in Guatemala and in Chile where she worked at the Swedish embassy in both countries. Lilian died of cancer in 2004.

Pato, Fransisco Pizarro
in our home

Lilian, Juancho and Tor
in serious conversations

After a while I started working at the Swedish Agency for Research Cooperation with Developing Countries (SAREC). I was responsible for, among other areas, research cooperation between Sweden and Cuba, so for a number of years I travelled to Cuba for work and took the opportunity to meet with Maria Elena and Nelson, as well as with Otilia, her husband Osvaldo and Patricia. Otilia later published a book about Dago and his four siblings, with the title "The dictatorship robbed me of five children"[68]. As long as she lived Otilia attempted to obtain clarification on the fate of her assassinated children. Patricia now lives in Chile, but her mental health is poor. The loss of all her siblings affected her permanently.

---

68 "La dictadura me arrebato cinco hijos" 1991

A couple who meant a lot to us as a family were Eliodoro Yáñez[69] and his wife Clarisa Arrieta, who were known by friends and family as "el Cuco" and "la Cuqita". They were an extraordinary older couple with hearts of gold, who had been very courageous after the coup. They had helped Juancho, together with other *compañeros,* by hiding them in their house, and when Juancho was arrested in their home, they were put under house arrest. They managed to escape when their guards were inattentive and after a few months of hiding the entered an embassy and then went on to live in exile in Paris. We visited them in Paris when our children were small, and they also came to see us in Sweden. The last time we saw them was when we went to Santiago for a visit in 1997.

Cuco and Cuquita in Paris 1989   My children Emilio, Isabel, Rossana and Daniel with Cuquita in Paris

69 Eliodoro was the grandson of a famous Chilean statesman by the same name, and his father was a well-known writer whose pseudonym was Juan Emar

Operation Condor and the following decades

During the first half of 1976 the situation in the countries of Latin America´s Southern Cone -Chile, Argentina, Paraguay, Bolivia, Brazil, and Uruguay – deteriorated further. In Argentina a military coup took place headed by General Jorge Videla. The general promised his contacts from the U.S. Central Intelligence Agency (CIA) that Argentina wouldn´t repeat the bloody persecution being practiced by Pinochet and his regime. The U.S. government, which supported Latin America´s so-called fight against communism, was grateful for this assurance as Chile´s transgressions of human rights were becoming a problem from an international perspective.[70] Gradually it became obvious that the Argentinian assurance wasn´t worth much; the difference was that the persecution was more silent, and worse. It became known as "the dirty war". No traces were left behind. The account of the number of assassinations by the military and secret services in Argentina is officially 30, 000, but it is highly probable that these numbers are heavily under-reported. The oppression and persecution in Argentina were thus far worse when compared to that of Chile. However, the dictatorship in Chile lasted for far longer and the changes it created and the institutional structure it consolidated has had a much greater impact on the whole of Chilean society.

Operation Condor, which became the system of cooperation between the secret services in the Southern Cone was formally established in November of 1976 but, in practice, this cooperation had already existed in a narrower sense between Chile and Argentina

---

70 See Dinges, John, "The Condor Years: How Pinochet and His Allies Brought Terrorism to Three Continents", The New Press, 2005

for a few years before. The cooperation was initiated by Pinochet and the head of DINA Manuel Contreras, and it included the secret services in Chile, Argentina, Uruguay, Paraguay, and Brazil.[71]

The U.S. was well aware of Operation Condor from the beginning and there are many documents on the U.S. activities in the Southern Cone. These were marked "classified" and kept secret for many years, but at last, in 1999, President Clinton ordered that all the classified documents related to Chile should be made public. Around 60 000 documents were de-classified, and, they became publicly available It was this event that led to Operation Condor becoming more widely known.

Operation Condor had three purposes: the first was to gather intelligence on "terrorists" in the Southern Cone; in reality people with Left sympathies; the second was to coordinate actions in order to be able identify and arrest "terrorists" in each individual country, as well as each other´s country; the third was to carry out assassinations of politicians that opposed the military dictatorships both within and outside the Southern Cone countries.

The CIA´s knowledge of these actions and its own participation in different ways in the dirty war in the Southern Cone has been thoroughly documented, and is now public. This participation was sanctioned at the highest levels. t has also been shown that Henry Kissinger, the then Secretary of State and National Security Adviser, supported the military regimes. John Dinges in his book, "The Condor Years: How Pinochet and His Allies Brought Terrorism to Three Continents" reveals how Kissinger respectively used a "red light, green light" system for his private meetings with military leaders and for public appearances. . In public he gave his support for the

---

71 All that follows that refers to Operation Condor comes from the above mentioned book by John Dinges

defense of human rights, while in private he assured the generals of U.S. support for their "fight against communism". Both Videla and Pinochet could therefore feel at ease with their continued assassination activities and plans. Operation Condor at the highest level was led by Pinochet, which also has been thoroughly documented.

Examples of the cooperation between the secret services in the Southern Cone, are the assassinationof General Prats, a minister in the Allende government, in Buenos Aires 1974; the assassination of Orlando Letelier, who also served as a minister in the Allende government and his colleague, Ronni Moffitt in Washington in 1975 and the failed assassination attempt against Bernardo Leighton, a Christian Democrat politician, in Rome 1975. The Uruguayan parliamentarians Zelmar Michelini and Héctor Gutiérrez Ruiz, as well as the former Bolivian president Juan José Torres were all assassinated by Operation Condor.

Miguel Enriquez´s brother, Edgardo Enriquez, was the foremost member of MIR who became a victim of the Argentinian secret services in cooperation with DINA. He was a member of the Political Commission.His political name was *Simon* and in the party his nickname was "El Pollo". Edgardo was MIR´s representative in the JCR and thus an important target for Operation Condor and was in Buenos Aires with the aim of returning to Chile. He was arrested on April 10, 1976, leaving a meeting of the JCR. After being tortured by the Argentinian secret service, he was turned over to DINA in Chile. After that he disappeared. His case was mentioned in the Rettig investigation in 1991. It was specifically taken up by the Spanish lawyer Baltasar Garzon in his indictment against Pinochet, which culminated in Pinochet's arrest in London many years later.

The worst of the blows against the JCR, apart from the arrest and murder of Edgardo Enriquez one year later, was the arrest in 1975 of Jorge Fuentes from MIR, Mario Santucho, the leader of the Argentinian PRT-ERP, and his brother Amilcar Santucho. Jorge was known within MIR as el *Trotsko,* "the Trotskist", They were travelling together for a JCR meeting with their Paraguayan counterparts. After months of torture in Paraguay, Jorge was handed over to DINA and has been disappeared ever since. Amilcar Santucho was released after some time in the Paraguayan jail.

In 1978 MIR initiated the Policy of Return. In practical terms leaders like Andrés Pascal, Arturo Villavela (*Coño Aguilar*) from the Political Commission and Patricio Rivas (*Gaspar*), Central Committee, together with others who had survived, returned to Chile underground. In total they numbered several hundred, and there were strict selection criteria for deciding which combatants were considered to fulfill the required prerequisites for return. It was not enough to just want to return. Sometimes they entered Chile deeply underground and didn´t leave the country for a long time. Sometimes they travelled back and forth from Chile on false passports. However not all survived. *Coño Aguilar* was identified in September 1983, when he was living in a house on Fuenteovejuna Street in Santiago and where he was shot to death in cold blood together with two other members of MIR. One of them was Lucia Vergara Valenzuela, *"la Piti"*, who I had gotten to know in Stockholm while shewas living there. Lucía was 31 at the time of her assassination. Arturo was 38.

Lucía had been married to José Benado Medvinsky, nicknamed " *Hippy*". He was one of the MIR members who had been imprisoned during the Frei government that preceded Allende. José had already returned to Chile in 1978 within the Policy of Return. He fell in 1980. By a curious coincidence he fell in the Samson´s farmhouse where I had hidden years before. Samson and Nana were also arrested but later released. José was kept in prison until 1983 and badly tortured. When he was released, he travelled to France where he was re-united with his two children. Lucía and José´s daughter Alexandra Benado Vergara who was born in 1976, was appointed as Minister of Sport in President Boric´s government in 2022.

During the ten years that passed from the military coup in September 1973, oppression and persecution by the military held the Chilean population in an iron grip, and the resistance suffered many losses. The dictatorship's economic policy was based on the so-called Chicago Boys formula, and its policies led, among other things, to the privatization of both the education and the health systems. As a consequence of these policies both the working class and the middle class suffered poverty as a consequence of these policies. The fall of the copper prices on the world market – copper being Chile´s main export product and thus a major source of income for the country – led to a widespread economic crisis in 1982, which in turn led to a political crisis within the right-wing alliance that supported the dictatorship. This political crisis opened up the possibility for mobilization among the most affected population.

During all the years of the dictatorship, there was a civil society organization that never stopped working and was active with hunger strikes and other protests. This was the "Agrupación de Familiares de Detenidos Desaparecidos" – AFDD (the Group of Families of the Detained and Disappeared). Under the wings of the Comité Pro Paz which had been created by the Catholic Church along with other churches, the AFDD was able to start working in a regular fashion at the end of 1974. With much courage and determination, the AFDD demanded to know the whereabouts of their loved ones tha had been detained and/or disappeared. The AFDD continues even today to demand justice and provide information, in order that no-one forgets.

From 1982 onwards major demonstrations against the dictatorship started to take place. Students, workers, women, and poor people from the shanty towns as well as the relatives of prisoners and the disappeared, took to the streets both to protest against the economic policy but also against the political oppression, in what came to be known as "Days of National Protest". The protests then continued sporadically, culminating in July 1986. MIR's paper "El Rebelde" was an active instrument in encouraging the protests and in disseminating information about them, togther with the Resistance Agency for Information ("Agencia Informativa de la Resistencia" – AIR) which had been created in 1980 and was an underground news agency. However neither MIR nor the other Left parties were capable of providing leadership to the protests. A number of military actions against Pinochet also took place around this time. Many of them were carried out by the Patriotic Front – Manuel Rodríguez ("Frente Patriotico Manuel Rodriguez")[72] which was an armed force with roots in the Communist Party.

Some years earlier, in 1980, MIR had installed a group of combatants in Neltume, in southern Chile, which is the same place where MIR had suffered a defeat right after the coup. MIR plans were for this group to be the start of a guerilla force in the rural areas. The group in Neltume was however discovered by the military and one year later it was annihilated. Armed actions were carried out by MIR after that,but these activities were gradually discontinued after 1983.

The total extent of the resistance has often been underestimated when Chile´s recent history has been told. This is partly because it was underground, and so little is known of its full extent. Even though the Left suffered heavy losses and defeat after the coup, the persistent resistance in different forms, including the armed actions during the 1980´s, undoubtedly contributed to the end of the dictatorship.[73]

---

72 Manuel Rodriguez was a hero from the Independence struggle against Spain
73 See "The forgotten history of the Chilean transition: armed resistance against Pinochet and U.S. Policy towards Chile in the 1980´s" by Victor Figueroa Clark

In accordance with the constitution that Pinochet had ordered, written, and then instituted in 1981, a referendum a referendum on the continuation of his presidency for a further eight years took place in in October 1988. This was the last step in a long process aimed at achieving the institutionalization of the military regime,which had started with the new constitution of 1981. Chile´s population answered with a resounding NO. As a result elections were held in 1989, which brought an end to the military regime. In 1990 Chile was able to start a slow and difficult transition to democracy, which more than thirty years later has yet to finalize.

This transition has largely been conducted by alliances between the center and the right. Since 1990 Chile has only experienced a limited form of democracy. Pinochet´s constitution together with some twenty laws of restriction ("leyes de amarre"), initially allowed the military a significant amount of influence in Congress and have severely limited democratic space. Pinochet had already in 1978 instituted laws that gave impunity to all military and secret service personnel. One example is the Amnesty Law (Ley de Amnistía 2191) for all those that participated in the repression between 1973-1978. Only in 2005 was it possible to make some reforms to Pinochet´s constitution but, its core elements are still in force today. Only when this constitution is completely replaced by another will it be possible to talk about a restoration of democracy.

The terrorism practiced by the military dictatorship against its own population only began to be documented by the Chilean state after 1991. The first investigation was the relatively limited Rettig investigation[74], after that there was the Valech investigation[75]. Yet another investigation, known as Valech II was initiated by president

74 "Informe de la Comisión Nacional de Verdad y Reconciliación" 1991 led by Raul Rettig
75 "Informe sobre Prisión Politica y Tortura" 2004 led by Sergio Valech

Michelle Bachelet in 2010. and, In its final report in 2011, the Valech II investigation documented that more than 40 000 people were victims of the military´s and secret service´s arrests and torture in its final report in 2011. Most of those who were arrested suffered gross abuse; many suffered immediately from torture; torture which frequently led to their deaths.

Ordinary detention facilities were obviously insufficient so many places that had other purposes such as sports stadiums, were initially used to place those who had been arrested. The most infamous of these was the National Stadium in Santiago. Many were arrested, let go, then re-arrested. The majority were never taken to court but just kept locked up, frequently being moved around and thenreleased, albeit often only after a number of years. Sometimes the former political prisoners were thrown out of the country and not given permission to return for a long time. Concentration camps were instituted. The most infamous among these were Isla Dawson, Tres Alamos, Cuatro Alamos, Ritoque, Puchuncaví, Chacabuco, Tejas Verdes and Colonia Dignidad, but there were many, many more all over the country. The Rettig investigation identified 1132 localities all over Chile, where torture and imprisonment had taken place.

There are however other estimates of the total number of deaths and torture during the dictatorship. According to Silvia Borzutzky in her book "Human Rights Policies in Chile – The Unfinished Struggle for Peace and Justice", official figures from 2015 state that around 4000 people were killed by the secret services and the military during the dictatorship. Her observation is that this number is most likely under-reported and that possibly as many as 25 000 were killed. An estimate of the number of people who were tortured could be as high as 100 000 according to trustworthy sources, while between 150 000 – 200 000 could have been detained for political reasons. According to Borzutzky between 200 000 and 400 000 Chileans went into exile.

In her book Borzutzky reports the case of the "Operation Removal of TVs" ("Operación Retiro de Televisores"). This was an order, given by Pinochet to the military, to get rid of bodies of prisoners who had been killed including the disappeared whose bodies have never been recovered. The order was that the bodies should be dug up from the mass graves into which they had been dumped, and then flown out to sea by big Puma helicopters and thrown into the ocean, in what came to be known as the Death Flights ("Vuelos de la Muerte"). Between 1974 and 1978 it has been estimated that between 400 – 500 bodies were thrown into the ocean in this manner. Many testimonies have been recorded from witnesses who participated in both the removals of dead bodies from mass graves and in the Death Flights themselves. They took place all over the country. Sometimes new mass graves were dug, and bodies dumped there instead of in the ocean, but few of these have so far been identified. These testimonies have subsequently been given in trials that have taken place after 2016.

As a result of the indictments against Pinochet initiated by the Spanish and Italian courts when he was visiting England in 1998, he was held under house arrest in London for 18 months until he was given permission to return to Chile for "health reasons". His so-called poor health was only a pretext for the conservative government of Margaret Thatcher to let him leave. On arriving at the airport in Santiago, Pinochet got up from his wheelchair and walked steadily to show off his good health. Although he had been released , the initiative by the European justice system led to the discovery of a legislative loophole that could be used by the Chilean justice system. The Chilean judge Juan Guzman Tapia discovered that the Amnesty Law didn´t cover kidnappings. In this way the Chilean justice system could slowly start to conduct trials against high-level military officers s as well as against those who had been active in the secret service. Trials were held and many guilty parties were given long prison sentences.

However, the democratically elected governments that followed from 1990 onwards were primarily concerned with the documentation of the truth about the dictatorship and its consequences, rather than with the dispensation of justice. The fear of provoking the military remained for a long time, and only when Pinochet retired as Chief of the Army and Head of the Armed forces did this fear start to fade. Up until 2015 only 10% of those that were guilty of assassinations and disappearances have been convicted, and only 2% of those that were guilty of torture.[76] The trials against the perpetrators have since continued slowly and are still taking place. One example is the case of the torturer and Assassin, Miguel Krassnoff, who was condemned again in his latest trial in 2024, has been condemned a total of 80 times and sentenced to a total of more than 1000 yea[7]r[7]s of prison.

The documentation of Operation Condor in the U.S. became the basis, together with anindictment in Chile against Pinochet on charges extensive fraud linked to the deposit of USD 13 million in an American bank in the U.S., for an arrest order to be issued against Pinochet in 2005. The indictment on crimes against human rights was dropped by the Chilean Supreme Court on the grounds that Pinochet's health was too poor for him to stand trial, but the indictment regarding fraud continued. Pinochet remained under house arrest and died in disgrace in December 2006.

---

76 Borzutzky "Human Rights Policies in Chile -The Unfinished Struggle for Truth and Justice"

77 See the digital Argentinian newspaper Infobae, July 1 , 2022

During the following years large street protests took place, such as the protests in 2006 carried out by the so-called Penguins ("Los Pinguinos"). The Penguins were high school students that were given this nickname due to their black-and-white school uniforms. Their protests were against the privatized school system which effectively excluded the poor population from access to education – an inheritance from the Pinochet Constitution. Large student protests then took place in 2008, 2011 and 2015 based on demands for a reform of the educational system. In October 2019 a different kind of protest took place, one which had an enormous impact through its extent and intensity. The apparently innocuous raise of the Metro tariff led to spontaneous protests, first by students, who were later joined by many people from both the working and the middle classes. The protests came to be known as the "Social Explosion" ("el Estallido Social"), and, at one point, 1.5 million people took part in a demonstration in the center of Santiago. Those that participated said that they had finally woken up to the oppression and exploitation that was still taking place thirty years after the socalled transition to a formal democracy. The protests were violently met by police – Carabineros – who were armed with firearms with rubber bullets which they shot with at close quarters. They aimed particularly at the demonstrators´ eyes, and as a result more than 400 people have lost their sight entirely or partially. 34 people died as a consequence of police violence.

The then conservative president Sebastian Piñera, publicly accused the protests of being a "declaration of war". The protests continued for two years and finally led to a national referendum in which the population were able to vote on whether they wanted a new constitution. The support for a new constitution was overwhelming. A process was initiated whereby a constitutional assembly ("asamblea constituyente") which was a group of 155 persons tasked with the drafting of a proposal for a new constitution, was elected. The assembly worked for more than a year and produced a radical and somewhat utopian proposal that was voted on, on September 4, 2022. It was mandatory to vote, and the majority (62%) rejected the proposal. There were a number of reasons for the rejection, among them an intense campaign from the right that spread lies and false messages, for example that the proposed constitution would turn Chile into a new Venezuela.

A second constitutional reform was elaborated by the Right and voted on in a referendum in December 2023, but this proposal was also rejected by a majority. There is a broad agreement that the Pinochet constitution should be replaced eventually, so formally the pre-requisites exist for a new reform attempt but the process is no stalled indefinitely. There is much apprehension and disillusionment concerning this whole issue. Meanwhile Pinochet´s constitution continues to be in place.

Pinochet´s shadow

On a personal level we, as a family, felt Pinochet´s dark shadow on us during the eighties and the nineties. A few months before the referendum in 1988 on the continuation of Pinochet´s rule, Juancho had to travel urgently to Chile so he could say farewell to his mother Doña Aída, who was very ill with cancer. As a family we had been in Buenos Aires at the start of the same year, and we had met with her and with Juancho´s father. During that visit which lasted three weeks, there were no signs of her illness, but upon returning to Chile she was diagnosed with cancer and became very ill soon after. Since the 15 years of exile that Juancho had been sentenced to had not yet been completed, he had to request a special permission to enter Chile on humanitarian grounds.

Juancho travelled to Santiago in July and was able to see his mother, but early one morning while he was still there in his parents´ home, a patrol car with armed men arrived and took him away. At the time I was in Sweden at my mother´s house in the south with the children. As soon as I got the phone call from Juancho´s relatives in Santiago telling me what had happened, I called the Swedish Ministry of Foreign Affairs to report that he had been kidnapped. By then Juancho was a Swedish citizen and since we were married and I was working at an Embassy abroad, he also carried a Swedish diplomatic passport. The kidnappers drove Juancho, blindfolded, around Santiago for some hours, taunting him for his stupidity in coming back to Chile, "being a wanted terrorist". Finally, they stopped by a park and told him to get out. He was told that he was going to be shot. Just as this was happening an order came on the walkie-talkie: to stop the execution. Juancho should not be shot. Instead, he was taken to the prison where his relatives were told that they could pick him up. They came to get him, and he went straight to the airport and took the first flight to Europe, arriving in Sweden soon after. I assume that the Swedish Embassy must have acted quickly when they had been informed by the Ministry of Foreign Affairs. Someone high up in the Chilean administration must have understood that it would be very detrimental to Pinochet´s image for a former political prisoner who was now Swedish citizen with a diplomatic passport to be assassinated in the center of Santiago a few months before the referendum.

Juancho´s life was saved but it was a close call.

Almost a decade later we were reminded that the secret service continued to exert an influence in the public administration in the "new democracy". The year was 1997 and we were going to travel as a family to spend time with Juancho´s relatives and friends in Santiago. Since I was worried for Juancho´s safety, even though the 15 years of exile had ended, I had warned a staff member at the Swedish Embassy in Santiago whom I knew personally that we were coming and given them our flight and arrival details. At this time I was working at the Swedish Embassy in Mozambique and had a diplomatic passport as did the children, but Juancho and I were divorced and he lived in Sweden as an ordinary citizen and was travelling on a normal passport.

We managed to coordinate our trips, so we all arrived together to the airport in Santiago. Juancho went first, no problem. Then the children, no problems. When it was my turn I was stopped. The immigration officer told me that I was on a list of people forbidden to enter the country. My name had been on this list since 1976 – twenty-one years earlier. I was informed that I needed to take the next plane leaving for Buenos Aires. I remember my children staring at me in panic from the other side of the passport control, wondering what was going on. I was allowed to make a phone call to the Swedish Embassy, so I could explain the situation and ask for their assistance. Meanwhile I refused to get on any departing plane. After a few hours an official from the Chilean Ministry of Foreign Affairs arrived and immediately reversed the order that had prevented me from entering the country. The official apologized profusely and assured me that my name was completely erased from the list. Our visit to Chile could continue as planned.

Final words

In the opinion of many, the resistance during the seventeen long years of dictatorship has often been tremendously underestimated, when accounts are given of the recent history of Chile. This in part is due to the clandestine nature, and therefore of the secrecy, of the resistance work and actions which has had as a consequence that the resistance in all its dimensions and coverage, is still largely undocumented and unknown. This void is also partly due to the fact that the reactionary media refrained from reporting on succesful resistance actions and only reported the blows against it. Although the forces within the Left suffered a heavy defeat after the coup, the organized resistance in a diversity of forms including the armed actions during the eighties, without any doubt, contributed to the end of the military dictatorship.

Now, many years later, when I finally have written down this account of what happened, there are so many feelings that come to the surface. It has been hard to write. I´m reminded of our feelings, both mine and Juancho´s, the first few years after we met. For a long time the heaviest feeling was one of sorrow for all of the *compañeros* and *compañeras* who lost their lives. A whole generation of brave young people who suffered indescribably and disappeared for ever. They have left behind an unimaginable void.

The sorrow over the defeat. The defeat that we in MIR and in the Resistance movement experienced and that weighed on us for many years after the deadly assault and persecution that the military implemented after the coup. We felt defeated, defeated by evil. It´s hard to convey how profound this feeling was. It was the sorrow over a vision that had been lost and over the huge human cost it entailed.

And then there was the feeling of survivors ´guilt, one that many others who have survived a war can recognize: why did *I* survive? What did I do to merit to continue living, when so many others – outstanding, brilliant, and incredibly brave *compañeros* and *compañeras* , lost their lives? There are no answers to this question.

It took a long time to come to terms with those feelings.

At the same time, I am reminded of my deep and lasting gratitude, and admiration for the brave people who helped me and hid me and other *compañeros*, at risk to their own lives.

Many challenges remain. Chile is still very much a class-based society with huge gaps between the well-to-do and the poor. The reactionary forces are still very strong and there is much frustration and suspicion from large groups of society towards the political parties and the politicians themselves. Corruption scandals associated with the top echelons of society including the Justice system have contributed to this lack of trust. Meanwhile the Left is divided and lacking in leadership.

Trials are still on-going against the perpetrators of the persecution during the dictatorship. However many questions remain unanswered, such as the whereabouts of the "disappeared".

In August 2023, ten days prior to the fifty years anniversary of the military coup, President Boric announced a national plan for the search and determination of the final destiny of the 1 162 identified "disappeared" persons (Plan Nacional de Busqueda de Verdad y Justicia). His plan is a commitment on the part of the Chilean State but a year on, there has been little progress.

Justice has thus not been fully served. The saying "justice delayed is justice denied" remains very true in Chile. Obviously there is a long road ahead before Chile can become a more egalitarian and just society.

The question remains: " Donde están? " (where are they?)

I have no doubts that the class struggle that has played out over the last fifty years, together with the endurance of the working class, of the most vulnerable and of the indigenous peoples as well as of the progressive forces within the middle class, mean that there is truly reason for hope. I welcome this and place my hope in the coming generations.

Stockholm October 2024

Bibliography

Allende´s Chile: the political economy of the rise and fall of the Unidad Popular by Stefan de Vylder (1976) Cambridge University Press, UK

"Chile: un largo septiembre" by Patricio Rivas (2006) Coedicion Ediciones Era, Mexico, LOM Ediciones, Chile

"Chile: massmobilisering och folkmakt 1970-1973" by Tor Sellström (1975) Unga Filosofers förlag, Sverige (in Swedish)

"El MIR vive en el corazón del pueblo: la lucha contra la burguesía y su prolongación democrática " by Nelson Gutierrez Yañez, (2018) Ediciones Escaparate, Chile

"El vuelo de la memoria" by Monica Echevarría (2002) LOM Ediciones, Chile

"Human Rights policies in Chile. The unfinished struggle for truth and justice" by Silvia Borzutzky (2015), Studies of the Americas, Institute of the Americas, University College, London. United Kingdom

"La dictadura me arrebató cinco hijos" by Otilia Vargas Vargas (1991) Edición Mosquito Comunicaciones, Chile

"Las Armas de Ayer" by Max Marambio (2007) Colección La Tercera-Debate, Random House Mondadori S.A., Chile

"MIR: dos años en la lucha de la Resistencia Popular del pueblo chileno 1973-1975" MIR (1976)

"The Condor Years" by John Dinges (2004) The New Press N.Y. USA

"Un día de octubre en Santiago" by Carmen Castillo (2013) Lom Ediciones Chile

Articles, thesis:

"El relato de la prensa mirista durante la dictadura cívico-militar 1973-1989" by Robinson Silva Hidalgo (2018) Dossier Izquierda, Chile

"Resistencia Politica popular en Chile: 1978-1984" by Robinson Silva Hidalgo

"Historia del MIR" by Cristián Perez, (2003) Estudios Públicos 2003, Chile

"Olvidos y Recuerdos de un montaje comunicacional" by María Olga Ruiz, 2014, Universidad de la Frontera, Chile

"The forgotten history of the Chilean transition: armed resistance against Pinochet and US Policy towards Chile in the 1980´s" by Victor Figueroa Clark, Cambridge University Press 2015

Public investigations in Chile:

"Informe de la Comisión Nacional de Verdad y Reconciliación", Raul Rettig et al 1991

Informe sobre Prisión Política y Tortura (Valech I), Sergio Valech 2004

Informe sobre Prisión Política y Tortura (Valech II), Maria Luisa Sepulveda 2011

Chilean Prosecutor´s accusation 28/02/2019

Proceso 1859

Causa Rol 16-2012: Regarding the assasination of Dagoberto Perez Vargas

Special Counsel on Violation of Human Rights in the Court of Appeals in San Miguel Minister Marianela Cifuentes